Little hands & Big hands

Huron Street Press proceeds support the American Library Association in its mission to provide leadership for the development, promotion, and improvement of library and information services and the profession of librarianship in order to enhance learning and ensure access to information for all.

Little hands & Big hands

Children and Adults Signing Together

KATHY MACMILLAN

Photographs by Kristin Brown

For
Gwendolyn -
Happy signing!
[ILY] Kathy MacMillan

an imprint of the American Library Association
HURON STREET PRESS
CHICAGO • 2014

Kathy MacMillan is a nationally certified American Sign Language interpreter who has taught basic American Sign Language to thousands of children, parents, and educators through interactive stories, songs, and games. Kathy is the author of *Try Your Hand at This! Easy Ways to Incorporate Sign Language into Your Programs* (Scarecrow Press, 2006) and *A Box Full of Tales* (American Library Association, 2008), and co-author of *Storytime Magic* (American Library Association, 2009), *Kindergarten Magic* (American Library Association, 2011), and *Multicultural Storytime Magic* (American Library Association, 2012). She was the library/media specialist at the Maryland School for the Deaf from 2001 to 2005, and prior to that she was a public children's librarian. She holds a Master of Library Science degree from the University of Maryland, College Park, and has been reviewing children's books and audiovisual materials for *School Library Journal* since 1999. Find her online at www.storiesbyhand.com.

Published by Huron Street Press, an imprint of ALA Publishing
Printed in the United States of America
18 17 16 15 14   5 4 3 2 1

ISBNs: 978-1-937589-39-4 (paper); 978-1-937589-40-0 (PDF). For more information on digital formats, visit the ALA Store at alastore.ala.org and select eEditions.

Library of Congress Cataloging-in-Publication Data

MacMillan, Kathy, 1975–
Little hands and big hands : children and adults signing together / Kathy MacMillan ; photographs by Kristin Brown.
pages cm
Includes bibliographical references and index.
ISBN 978-1-937589-39-4 (alk. paper)
1. Sign language. 2. Sign language acquisition—Parent participation. 3. Nonverbal communication in children. 4. American Sign Language. I. Title.
HV2474.M318 2014
372.6—dc23   2013011538

Cover and text design by Kimberly Thornton in Caecilia, Gotham, and Chapparal Pro.
Cover photograph © Lori Sparkia /Shutterstock, Inc.

♾ This paper meets the requirements of ANSI/NISO Z39.48-1992 (Permanence of Paper).

contents

acknowledgments

This book couldn't have happened without the willingness of the following creative, talented people to put up with me:

Kristin Brown, who let me bully her into this
Stephanie Zvirin, who launched the ship
Christine Schwab, who navigated it
Carolyn Crabtree, who watched for icebergs
Kimberly Thornton, who created a beautiful design
Louise Rollins, who knows more about early childhood development than anyone I've ever met, and never lets all that knowledge get in the way of having fun with kids
Christine Kirker, who keeps the creative fires burning
And last but definitely not least, JX MacMillan, sign model and son extraordinaire, who lets me test all my wacky ideas on him

introduction

When my son, James Xavier (JX for short), was born in 2005, the decision to sign with him was the most natural thing in the world—after all, I was an American Sign Language interpreter and had been working with both deaf and hearing children as a public and school librarian for years. I had seen firsthand how kids of all ages responded to sign and how even six-month-old babies could communicate their needs through signs. I started signing with him literally hours after his birth, looking forward to the many benefits it would bring to him: enhanced self-esteem, earlier communication, maybe even a higher IQ.

But let's be honest: the number one reason I wanted to sign with JX was to make our lives easier. After all, if he could tell me what he wanted instead of crying, wouldn't that make life less frustrating for both of us? In my enthusiasm I even added a new series of classes to the sign language storytelling classes I offered for children—"Little Hands Signing," designed to share the benefits of signing with babies, toddlers, and preschoolers through age-appropriate books, music, activities, and fingerplays.

JX, like every child, is determinedly himself. Whatever the books said, he wasn't going to sign his first sign until he was good and ready—and that turned out to be at the age of fourteen months, long after I had begun to despair of his ever signing back to me. And then he signed three signs in rapid succession, and in a few days had tripled his signing vocabulary. He enthusiastically picked up new signs and happily taught them to his grandparents and friends. At age three, despite my determination not to push him to read too early, he taught himself to read. Now that he's in second grade, he can't get enough chapter books and reports that his favorite day of the week is Library Day.

I share this not to brag about my kid (though, like any mom, I am happy to talk about how amazing he is!), but to point out what can happen when a child is constantly surrounded with language and interaction—he becomes interested in words, in literacy, in communication. In this book, I attempt to rectify what I see as a shortcoming of many books on signing with babies and young children: they present signing with children in a vacuum, as if signing is a magical device that will produce a well-adjusted, intelligent, successful child. In fact, signing with young children is so valuable because it can work in concert with stories, nursery rhymes, games, discipline techniques, and more to help your child process and communicate about everyday experiences.

Additionally, many books about signing with children assume that parents will stop signing once their child begins to speak, when in fact many families have discovered the enormous benefits of expanding their signing repertoire throughout preschool, elementary school, even middle and high school. This book is designed to give enough of the basics for beginners to get started, but also to offer more advanced activities for families who have been signing with their children for awhile and want more. I bring three different perspectives to this book: that of an interpreter, fluent in American Sign Language; that of a librarian and educator experienced with engaging children in early literacy; and that of a mom who knows the frustrations and joys of living every day with a young child. Our focus here is on practical applications of the signs you can use every day to make your life with your child both easier and more fulfilling.

chapter 1

Why Sign?

Signing with Your Baby or Toddler

THE NUMBER ONE REASON THAT PARENTS CHOOSE to sign with their babies is that babies can sign long before they can speak. Because the muscles in the hands develop much more quickly than those that control the voice box, babies can produce signs as young as six or seven months old and can begin to connect signs to concepts long before that. Signing can reduce frustration for parents, who no longer have to wonder what the baby wants, and also for the child, who is no longer trapped in a world of one-way communication.

Learning to communicate effectively with other people is the most important accomplishment in your child's life. Even the youngest babies communicate their desires, needs, and frustrations through coos, cries, squeals, and movement. Children who don't learn to communicate may become isolated and rejected as they grow up (Weitzman and Greenberg 2002).

Some detractors worry that signing with babies will delay their speech. In fact, research shows the opposite to be true; one study found that two-year-olds whose parents had signed with them had an average of fifty more words in their spoken vocabularies, compared to toddlers whose parents had not signed with them. By age three, the children who had signed as babies spoke at a level almost an entire year ahead of the nonsigners (Briant 2004). This outcome is due to the cyclical nature of parent-child communication—a baby or toddler who signs is able to start a conversation on a topic that interests him, which then prompts the adult to speak about the topic. The child, already engaged in the topic, pays close attention and absorbs the spoken words, which enhance his spoken language development.

Signing with young children can also increase their self-esteem. The simple act of being able to communicate increases confidence and security. Think of the empowering message you are sending to your child when you give her the tools to communicate: "What you have to say is valuable, and I want to listen." In addition, signing requires eye contact and attention—and so is perfect for encouraging the kind of engagement that young children need from adults for healthy development.

Signing with Your Preschooler

Although some caregivers may view signing with children as a means to an end—the end being to develop speech—there are many benefits to continuing to sign with a child once he or she is speaking. After all, many young children may have difficulty pronouncing some words (or their parents may have difficulty understanding them!) so telling a frustrated child to "Use your signs" can defuse tantrums and restore communication.

There are practical benefits as well: you can sign across a room or through a window. You can sign underwater. You can discreetly ask a child whether he needs to use the restroom or, without even opening your mouth, make it clear that a certain behavior will not be tolerated. I found signing especially useful when my son started swim lessons at age three. The parents were told to sit on the observation deck above the pool. He didn't like the distance at first, but when he realized he could sign to me whenever he wanted, his anxiety evaporated!

Signing stimulates multiple senses, so it is an ideal companion to early literacy. It enhances word recognition, and, combined with speech, builds the visual, auditory, and kinesthetic centers of the brain. The active nature of signing engages energetic young children and helps them focus. One study found that first graders' spelling improved from 25–46 percent accuracy to 56–90 percent accuracy simply by adding fingerspelling (signing letters in American Sign Language) to their spelling practice (Hafer and Wilson 1986). Why? Young children learn best through play, and signing makes learning more playful.

Signing with Your Special Needs Child

All the benefits discussed so far also apply to children with special needs. However, in the case of a child with a special need, it may be imperative to provide your child with a painless means of communication. All children need to be exposed to competent language models in order to develop language and literacy skills. Although it's natural to focus on the physical and environmental adaptations that your child needs, don't forget to adapt communication as well. As one mother of a deaf child writes, "You do not grow a cactus in the rain forest" (Frazier-Maiwald and Williams 1999). Although your ultimate goal may be to ensure that your child functions well in a mainstream environment, remember that your child also needs effective communication and language development *now*. Signing is often the key to social interaction for children with special needs.

Deaf and hard-of-hearing children. Although many technological interventions are available for deaf and hard-of-hearing children, none takes the place of communication and language. For a child with a hearing loss, sign language is simply the most comfortable way to communicate, using the child's strengths instead of her weaknesses. Without a strong foundation in a first language, children cannot learn a second or third language. For deaf and hard-of-hearing children in the United States, American Sign Language (ASL) is the most accessible first language. Developing proficiency in ASL gives children the early language skills to learn English (spoken, written, or both) as a new language. If your child is deaf or hard-of-hearing, the activities in this book may be useful to you, but they should not take the place of exposing your child (and yourself!) to fluent ASL language models. You may want your child to speak, but be careful not to send the message that speaking correctly is more important than having something to say!

Children with learning disabilities. Research indicates that using signs with children with dyslexia and other learning disabilities can help overcome processing problems related to reading and spelling (Hafer and Wilson 1986). Children benefit because signing associates movement with the concepts, integrates the senses into learning, and combats boredom by offering a new perspective on classroom material.

Children with Down syndrome or autism. Using signs with children with Down syndrome can support and enhance verbal skills. When the child signs, parents begin to understand what the child is saying, and they talk back, thereby exposing the child to a wider vocabulary. Children on the autism spectrum tend to process information better when it is presented visually, and so signing is ideal. Signing also reinforces and supports speech development (Daniels 2001).

Children with speech delays. Most children begin speaking between ten and eighteen months of age, but approximately 10 percent of children have a speech or language delay (Bingham 2007). Although human beings can live a completely fulfilled life without speech, as evidenced by many successful Deaf adults, it is impossible to do so without language. Therefore, a language delay is much more serious than a speech delay. Effective communication is the most important skill a young child can develop. For children with speech delays, signing provides a way to interact with others and promotes the development of speech by taking the frustration and anxiety out of communication.

About American Sign Language

American Sign Language is the language used by the Deaf communities of the United States and Canada. Like other sign languages throughout the world, it is a real language with its own grammar, syntax, and culture. Unfortunately, some baby sign language books and programs have chosen to use made-up gestures in place of signs. The producers of these materials often feel that true sign languages are too difficult for children to produce or for parents to learn, or perhaps they themselves lack the fluency to understand and identify appropriate signs for children. This use of made-up gestures is problematic for several reasons:

- Using made-up gestures deprives children of the brain-building benefits of exposure to real languages.
- On a practical level, made-up gestures are the equivalent of a secret code between you and your child. Although this activity may be helpful in the short term, it will not allow your child to communicate with others.
- The claim that signs are too hard for babies is simply untrue. After all, both deaf and hearing children of deaf parents have been learning to sign very effectively for hundreds of years. Although it is true that *some* signs are difficult for babies to produce, the same is true of vocabulary in every language on earth. Young children may sign some signs in a nonstandard way while learning, just like they might mispronounce some spoken words. This is simply how young children acquire language.
- Sometimes the made-up gestures advanced by these products are offensive in American Sign Language, unbeknownst to the well-meaning parents who teach these gestures to their children.
- The vast majority of baby sign language materials are purchased by hearing, non-signing parents who don't know how to evaluate the signs. The producers of these materials know this, which makes their decision not to use a true sign language even more irresponsible.
- Because more and more deaf children are being mainstreamed into public schools, your child will likely have a deaf classmate at some point. Learning even a few ASL signs now may open a door to communication with a new friend in the future.
- ASL is commonly cited as the third or fourth most used language in the United States. (Because of imprecise census questioning, this figure is difficult to pinpoint.)
- As an actual language, ASL stimulates the language centers of the brain in a way that made-up gestures do not.

- Imagine writing a book about teaching French to children and insisting, "French pronunciation is too hard for babies. Just make noises like Pepe Le Pew instead." The practice of using made-up gestures displays just such disrespect to American Sign Language and the Deaf culture that cherishes it.

To reap the full benefits of signing with your child, make sure that any book, DVD, or other product you use states that it uses American Sign Language.

chapter 2

The Developing Child, the Developing Brain

THE FIRST FIVE YEARS OF LIFE ARE CRUCIAL FOR A child's cognitive, emotional, and social development because the brain is still developing. In fact, the brain is the only organ that is not complete at birth. During the first five years of life, the synapses, or pathways between the nerve cells in the brain, develop at an astounding rate, with one thousand trillion synapses forming in the first eight months alone. As a child experiences the world, the synapses that receive the most stimulation become stronger, while those with little or no stimulation are pruned away. The pruning process speeds up around age one, as the brain develops the most efficient "wiring" based on the stimulation it receives. Therefore, a child who is *not* exposed to effective language and communication in the first years of life may lose the mental flexibility and capacity to develop effective language later. Conversely, by exposing young children to engaging, quality language and communication in the formative years, we lay the foundation for later language learning and literacy.

The following summary of developmental milestones provides a broad overview of basic child development. Children may vary widely depending upon their environment, genetics, and special needs. An individual child may also develop at different rates in different areas.

From birth to three months, a baby is just beginning to discover the world. He can see faces in his immediate line of vision, as when he is being fed. Babies at this stage look around alertly and will go quiet at the sound of a familiar voice. They will coo and gurgle, but they are not yet aware that sounds have meaning. By the end of this period, babies typically can hold up their heads and enjoy playing with their hands and fingers. They will also begin to copy simple movements and facial expressions, laying the foundation for communication and social awareness. At this stage, the brain is forming mental connections quickly and is organized to take in sounds and gestures of any type, including those not found in the child's native language.

From three to six months, babies begin to interact with the world more by turning toward sounds, smiling, laughing, crying to express emotion, and babbling with single sounds, such as "buh" or "mah." They begin to develop hand-eye coordination—for example, by seeing a toy and then reaching for it. Their eyesight develops, and they can now see and track things in their environment and can see things farther away. Babies are especially interested in faces—they can recognize familiar people by sight, and they like looking in mirrors. By the end of this stage, most babies can pass objects from one hand to the other. Here the brain begins the long process of pruning language synapses to recognize only familiar sounds (those in the language[s] the child has heard or seen often). This is why young children can produce foreign languages without an accent—their brains are still able to recognize and produce sounds or gestures that adults' brains have pruned away.

From six to nine months, babies begin to string sounds together in their babbling (for example, "mamamama" instead of just "mah") and become interested in copying the sounds and gestures made by others. Babies may also "sign babble" at this stage, using repetitive motions such as opening and closing the hands. In babies who are not exposed to sign language, this gestural babbling will eventually stop. In those who are exposed to signing, these repetitive gestures will eventually develop into signs just as spoken babbling will develop into words. Many babies who have been exposed to signs will begin to sign back at this point. In this stage, babies start to become aware that something exists even if it is hidden, and they may become interested in games like peek-a-boo or hide-the-toy. At just eight months of age, babies begin to understand words or signs out of their usual context.

From nine to twelve months, babies begin to interact with others more, perhaps by putting out an arm or leg to help with dressing, by using signs or sounds to get attention, or even by speaking simple words. Distinct personalities and preferences begin to emerge, and babies may assert those preferences by insisting on a certain toy or book or by crying when a favorite person leaves. Babies at this age can respond to simple verbal or signed requests. As they continue to become attuned to the rhythms of speech, their babbling takes on the tones of spoken language, even if the words are incomprehensible. They continue to copy words and gestures and explore things in their environment in new ways, perhaps by throwing or banging.

Many babies will produce their first signs during this time and may have a sign vocabulary of about ten signs by the age of one year.

From twelve to eighteen months, toddlers expand their interactions with others even more. They like to hand things to other people, show affection, and point, sign, or talk to share interesting things with other people. At this age, children may begin to explore their environment alone but generally still like to have a caregiver close by. By the age of eighteen months, most children can say several individual words and use them to communicate basic needs and wants. They can also follow simple, one-step verbal commands such as "give me the book." Signing toddlers may begin to combine signs into sentences, such as "WANT BOOK" or "MORE MILK PLEASE." They may also sign some letters of the alphabet, and they may have a signing vocabulary of up to forty signs, though they will likely understand many more.

From eighteen months to two years, children develop more independence and become very interested in other children. They do not quite know how to play with other children yet, however, and they may play beside them instead. They love to copy others, especially older children and adults. At this age, children may assert their growing sense of independence by becoming defiant. By age two, most children can say simple two- to four-word sentences, follow two-part directions, and point to objects or pictures when they are named. Signing toddlers will likely have a vocabulary of twenty or more signs at the beginning of this stage and may sign two hundred or more signs by age two. They begin to sort shapes and colors and may engage in pretend play. They may also begin to use one hand more than the other. Physically, children at this age develop very quickly, learning how to kick a ball, run, climb, walk up and down stairs, and stand on tiptoe.

From two to three years, children become more aware of the feelings of others and may show concern when a friend is upset. They continue to copy others naturally, and come to understand the concepts of taking turns and sharing. At this age, children enjoy structure and routines and may need extra help transitioning if a routine is disrupted. Linguistically, they can understand and follow three-part directions and generally can speak well enough for strangers to understand them most of the time, using multiple sentences. At this age, children may even sign basic fingerspelled words, but they do not yet understand that these words are made up of separate letters—they see the word as a single sign. Children at this age understand basic number concepts, can do simple puzzles, and become interested in pretend play. Physical development continues as children become skilled climbers and runners and can walk up and down stairs with one foot on each step.

From three to four years, children enjoy learning and doing new things, and their play becomes more associated with make-believe. They are very interested in playing with other children and begin to develop cooperation skills. By age four, most children willingly discuss things they are interested in, can recite songs or poems from memory, and begin to use grammar correctly. They know basic colors and numbers and can make predictions about what will happen next in stories. By age four, most children begin to understand that there is a difference between what they know and what someone else knows. Physically, they develop the ability to perform activities that require the hemispheres of the brain to coordinate, such as hopping or standing on one foot.

From four to six years, children become very interested in having, being like, and pleasing their friends. They are also likely to be eager followers of rules, and they become very aware of their gender. They can easily tell the difference between what is real and what is imaginary, and they show even more independence. Most children speak very clearly by age five and can tell a simple story coherently, making correct use of tenses. Five-year-olds generally can count to ten or higher and can print some letters or numbers. Their physical abilities develop further, allowing them to stand on one foot for ten seconds or more, hop and skip, and properly use a fork and spoon. By age six, a dominant hand has been established in most children, and they can perform basic fine motor actions such as reaching, grasping, and carrying things.

This chapter synthesizes information from the following sources: California School for the Deaf 2005; French 1999; Mayes and Cohen 2002; Ontario Ministry of Children and Youth Services 2010; Shelov and Altmann 2009; and Shonkoff and Phillips 2000.

chapter 3

Signing and Early Literacy

What Is Early Literacy?

THE MOST IMPORTANT POINT TO UNDERSTAND ABOUT early literacy is that it does not mean early reading. In fact, children who are subjected to direct teaching of reading and writing before they are developmentally ready are more likely to be diagnosed with ADHD, dyslexia, and other learning disabilities (Johnson 2007). Early literacy skills are the components of communication that lay the groundwork for language development and later literacy skills. By exposing your child to a wide variety of positive experiences with language and books, you provide a solid foundation for the reading and writing skills to come.

The National Institute of Child Health and Human Development identifies six key early literacy skills:

1. **Print motivation:** interest in books and printed materials
2. **Phonological awareness:** the ability to hear and play with smaller sounds in words
3. **Vocabulary:** knowing and understanding words
4. **Narrative skills:** the ability to describe things and tell stories
5. **Print awareness:** noticing print, knowing how to hold a book and turn pages, knowing how to follow words on a page
6. **Letter knowledge:** Knowing the letters of the alphabet and their sounds in spoken English (Ghoting and Martin-Diaz 2005)

How Signing Enhances Early Literacy

Whenever you communicate with your child in an involving way, you are helping her develop early literacy skills. Because signing encourages communication and engagement, it supports early literacy. But that's not the only way signing helps your child develop language and literacy skills. In her groundbreaking book, *Dancing with Words: Signing for Hearing Children's Literacy* (2001), Marilyn Daniels describes her research on using American Sign Language in preschool classrooms with hearing children. More often than not, her research was disrupted when the parents of her control group (a preschool classroom where the teacher was *not* using sign language with the students) heard about the amazing gains the signing classrooms in the study were making and insisted that their children be exposed to sign too! She found that hearing preschoolers and kindergartners in the signing groups achieved significantly higher scores on the Peabody Picture Vocabulary Test than did those who knew no signs. In addition, teachers in the signing classrooms reported that their students were less frustrated, got along better, and were more excited about learning than students in their previous, non-signing classes.

How did signing with these groups produce such extraordinary results?

- Sign language supports different learning styles. Signs provide a visual cue and give kinesthetic learners, who learn best through physical activity, a way to interact with letters and vocabulary.
- Knowing the names of the letters of the alphabet is an important first step on the road to literacy. Using the manual alphabet with children helps them learn, remember, and use the letters—long before they have developed the fine motor skills to write them clearly.
- As children move into the preschool and early elementary years, knowing signs and the manual alphabet allows them to access two different "memory stores" in their brains for reading, spelling, and vocabulary. For example, if a child cannot identify a letter's sound, signing it to himself may help jog his memory to make the connection.
- American Sign Language, like any language, stimulates the language centers of the brain, strengthening synaptic connections and preparing them for further language learning.
- Young children tend to be more visually attuned than adults, and so signing to them naturally captures their attention. In addition, our visual sense works best when our eyes are moving, as when we are observing signs.
- The areas of the brain that control movement develop earlier than those that control speech. Because of this development, even six- to seven-month-old babies can produce signs. As children grow up, their motor centers continue to develop ahead of their speech centers, allowing them to express more thoughts more clearly through signs than they can through speech.

- Adults tend to use writing as a way to process and understand information. Young children do not have access to this tool yet, but they can use signs to serve the same function.
- ASL signs can help children understand and remember meaning. Many ASL signs are iconic, meaning that they look like what they mean. For example, the sign ELEPHANT looks like the trunk of an elephant. Many more signs are arbitrary, meaning that the form of the sign has no relation to the meaning but may help children make sense of the meaning of a word nonetheless. For example, the sign SORRY is made by using the S-handshape and moving it in a circle over the heart, accompanied by an apologetic expression. Although this sign would not be immediately understood by someone who did not know American Sign Language, it incorporates the *s* that is the first letter of the English word *sorry*, and it takes place at the heart, indicating that emotion is involved.

ELEPHANT: Hold a flat hand at the nose and move it down and away from you to show the shape of an elephant's trunk.

SORRY: Make a fist and move it in a circle over your heart. Make sure your facial expression shows that you are sorry!

- The hands are connected to the brain. Developing the tactile sense (touch) and the kinesthetic sense (movement) helps the different hemispheres of the brain communicate with one another, allowing for more seamless processing of information.
- Before children can understand the abstract shapes of letters, they must first develop their proprioceptive system, or a sense of where they are in space. When a child moves, proprioceptive development is triggered as muscles, joints, and tendons make contact and brain connections develop (Johnson 2007). The movement of signs naturally encourages proprioceptive development.

BEST BOOKS FOR EVERY AGE

BIRTH TO SIX MONTHS

- Cardboard books with bold patterns in black and white or primary colors
- Cloth books
- Bath books
- Books about people and familiar objects
- Wordless picture books
- Nursery rhyme books

SIX TO TWELVE MONTHS

- Board books with pictures of babies
- Texture books
- Cloth books
- Bath books
- Homemade books with pictures of family and friends
- Small books that fit into the child's hand
- Books about the body
- Books that encourage the child to repeat a refrain
- Nursery rhyme books

TWELVE TO EIGHTEEN MONTHS

- Books about actions and basic concepts such as opposites
- Texture books
- Cloth books
- Bath books
- Homemade books with pictures of family and friends
- Books about the body and everyday routines
- Books that ask questions for the child to answer
- Books with simple, predictable stories
- Nursery rhyme books

EIGHTEEN TO TWENTY-FOUR MONTHS

- Books with more complex pictures
- Books about topics your child is interested in
- Wordless picture books
- Books about common experiences
- Nursery rhyme books
- Books about feelings

TWO TO THREE YEARS

- Simple rhymes children can memorize
- Nursery rhyme books
- Wordless picture books
- Books about concepts
- Books about favorite characters
- Books about topics your child is interested in
- Books about common experiences

THREE TO FOUR YEARS

- Poetry
- Nursery rhyme books
- Wordless picture books
- Books about concepts
- Books about favorite characters
- Books about topics your child is interested in
- Books with refrains your child can repeat with you
- Simple folktales
- Stories with more complex narrative structure

FOUR TO SIX YEARS

- Poetry
- Nursery rhyme books
- Wordless picture books
- Books about concepts
- Books about favorite characters
- Books about topics your child is interested in
- Books about children around the world
- Stories with more complex narrative structure
- Folktales
- Books about feelings and social interactions

Adapted from Caroline J. Blakemore and Barbara Weston Ramirez, *Baby Read-Aloud Basics* (New York: AMACOM, 2006), and Zero to Three, "Early Literacy" (2003), www.zerotothree.org/child-development/early-language-literacy/earlyliteracy2pagehandout.pdf.

Signing in itself seems to be intrinsically motivating for children; as one United Kingdom study reports, "Children's motivation for acquiring basic signing skills does not appear to stem from interaction with Deaf children or adults as much as from the language itself" (Daniels 2003).

Signing with children facilitates a sense of play. Play is far more than just simple entertainment—it is the number one way children learn about the world in the first five years of life. Play allows children to make connections between concepts and understand how the pieces of the world fit together—and if children figure these things out for themselves, the resulting brain connections last far longer than if children receive direct instruction.

Reading and Signing with Your Child

Signing is a natural and fun way to engage your child in books and reading. This book contains many suggestions for incorporating rhymes, songs, read-alouds, and language games throughout your day, and each section also features theme-related book recommendations. You can also incorporate signs into any book you read with your child. Reading aloud with children exposes them to a wider vocabulary than they hear in everyday conversation, encourages discussion and interaction, and promotes bonding between parent and child.

When reading to your child, use signs to emphasize key concepts, to make connections, or simply to reinforce vocabulary. You can use signs with any book, but certain types of books lend themselves especially well to signing. In her 2004 book, *Baby Sign Language Basics*, Monta Z. Briant identifies three types:

1. Books with a single concept on each page, such as *We Went Walking* by Sue Williams. Use the signs for the key concepts.
2. Books that use a refrain, such as *Bear Wants More* by Karma Wilson. Encourage your child to sign the refrain with you.
3. Books with pictures of everyday objects. Use signs to help your child explore the pictures and expand his vocabulary.

Eight Tips for Reading Aloud with Your Child

1. Share books every day. This activity tells your child that reading is important.
2. Read with expression. Make the words come alive!
3. Before you start the story, show the cover and discuss what the book is about. This models pre-reading and prediction skills.

4. Let your child turn the pages and be involved in the story.
5. Make connections between the story and your child's life.
6. Stop to ask questions or interact with your child throughout the story.
7. Don't worry if your child can't sit still for a whole story—follow her lead and keep storytime fun. It's okay to stop in the middle, skip around, or go back and repeat favorite parts.
8. Read the same book over and over (and over and over . . .) if your child asks for it. Children thrive on repetition; if a child asks for a book again and again, there is something important that he is learning from it or processing in it.

Building Blocks of Language

Sara Bingham identifies the "building blocks of language" as shared attention, turn taking, and vocabulary growth (Bingham 2007). Any time you are focusing on the same thing as your child, communicating about it, dialoguing about it, and exposing your child to language, you are promoting her language development. Parents all around the world naturally use an exaggerated form of language known as "parentese" or "child-directed speech" when speaking to babies and young children—you probably do it without even thinking about it! But research shows that parentese actually helps young children process language by drawing their attention to important features of language (Blakemore and Ramirez 2006). Parentese exists in every language, including sign languages.

FEATURES OF PARENTESE/CHILD-DIRECTED SPEECH

In Spoken Languages

- Adult's face held close to baby's face
- Short sentences
- Singsong tone
- Clear articulation
- Higher pitch
- Repetition for emphasis and reinforcement
- Exaggerated facial expression
- Lengthening of vowels
- Longer pauses
- Placement of unfamiliar words at the end of the sentence to emphasize them
- Less complex grammatical structures
- Positive feedback

In Signed Languages

- Adult's face held in baby's line of sight
- Short sentences
- Higher ballisticality (tension in wrists when producing signs)
- Holding signs longer
- Larger sign space
- Repetition for emphasis and reinforcement
- Exaggerated facial expression
- Slower pacing
- Longer pauses with continued eye contact
- Less complex grammatical structures
- Positive feedback

chapter 4

Signing in Action

THIS BOOK IS A RESOURCE FOR INCORPORATING signs into literacy-building stories, songs, and games with children and for engaging them with language at multiple levels. This book is not a catchall beginner's guide to signing with young children; that's why, for example, you won't find all of baby's favorite food signs listed in the "Mealtime" section. If you're new to signing with your child, you will find lots of fun activities here, and you can also find many great books about the basics of signing with babies and toddlers in appendix A, "More Resources for Signing with Young Children."

When to Start

It's never too early, or too late, to start signing with your child. Although some researchers have found babies signing back as young as four months old, most don't sign until at least six or seven months of age—and some, even with constant exposure, produce their first signs much later (Brady 2000). Whatever your child's age, she will benefit from being exposed to signs, just as she benefits from being exposed to words.

If you are just beginning to sign with your baby, start with these three signs, guaranteed to make your life easier:

MORE is an excellent first sign, as it can apply to just about anything your child wants more of: food, cuddling, music, tickling, reading, and so on.

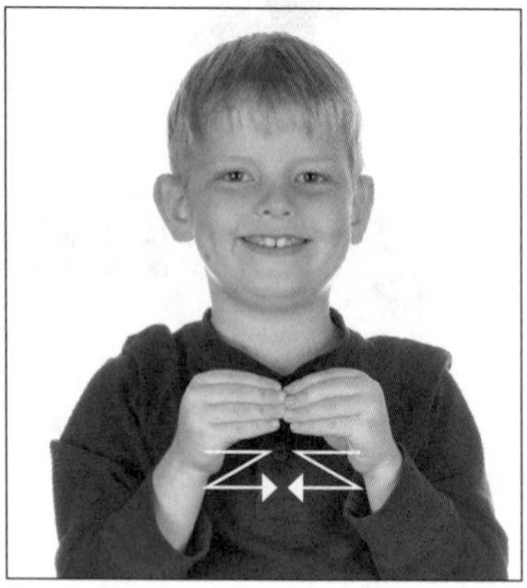

MORE: Tap gathered fingertips and thumbs of each hand together.

An ideal companion to MORE, ALL-DONE lets your child tell you when he has had enough of something. You can also use it in many different ways if you alter your facial expression:

- With eyebrows up: "Are you all done?"
- Neutral facial expression: "That activity is done now."
- Stern facial expression and sharper movement: "Knock it off!"

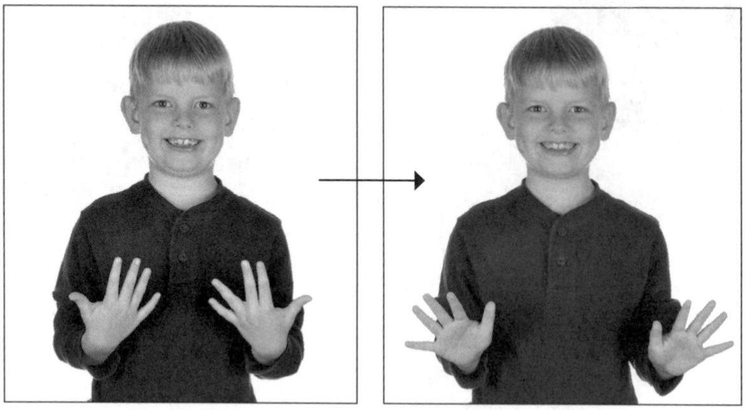

ALL-DONE: Hold flat hands facing you and then turn them to face outward.

Given its important role in babies' lives, MILK is a no-brainer!

MILK: Hold one hand as if milking a cow and squeeze the udder.

Stages of Signing Development

BIRTH TO THREE MONTHS

Is drawn to movement
Looks attentively at faces

THREE TO SIX MONTHS

May "babble" with the hands
Begins to understand that signs have meaning in specific contexts
Begins to make eye contact
May imitate facial expressions
Points to people, objects, and places

SIX TO TWELVE MONTHS

May "babble" with the hands
Begins to understand signs out of context
Begins to understand that signs have meaning
May produce first sign
May have a vocabulary of ten or more signs by the end of this period
Enjoys clapping and repetitive rhythms
Begins to respond to signed requests

TWELVE TO EIGHTEEN MONTHS

Begins to produce two-sign phrases
Expands sign vocabulary
May use simple fingerspelling (or approximations of fingerspelling)
May produce signs using approximations of more difficult handshapes

EIGHTEEN TO TWENTY-FOUR MONTHS

Begins to produce three-sign phrases
May have a vocabulary of two hundred or more signs by the end of this stage

TWO TO THREE YEARS

Begins to follow social cues, becoming interested in things simply because others are interested in them
Uses signs to clarify spoken words
May use signs alone to express self when feeling overwhelmed, tired, or frustrated
Continues to expand sign vocabulary

THREE TO FOUR YEARS

Shows preference for right or left hand
Continues to expand sign vocabulary

FOUR TO SIX YEARS

Develops bilateral hand skills (may sign with alternate hands); has generally established dominant hand by the end of this period
Can perform basic fine motor activity such as reaching, grasping, and manipulating objects in the hand
Can sign most ASL handshapes correctly
Continues to expand sign vocabulary

This section synthesizes information from the following sources: California School for the Deaf 2005; Frazier-Maiwald and Williams 1999; Garcia 1999; Isbell 2010; and Miller 2007.

Helpful Hints

1. START SLOW AND CHOOSE SIGNS THAT MATTER TO YOUR CHILD.

Young children are wired to acquire language in whatever form we give it to them, so you can't overwhelm your baby or toddler with too many signs any more than you can overwhelm her with too many words. But it *is* possible to overwhelm yourself if you try to learn too many signs at once! Start with signs that motivate your child or that relate directly to everyday routines; the activities in chapter 5 fall into this category.

2. BE CONSISTENT AND REPEAT OFTEN.

"*Intensity*, *frequency*, and *duration* are the keys to development," writes Margaret Sasse, author of *Active Baby, Healthy Brain* (2009). Consistency not only provides continual reinforcement of what your child is learning but also allows your child to develop a sense of security, without which real learning cannot happen.

WHAT BABIES KNOW

Dr. Joseph Garcia (1999) lists these basic concepts as the first that babies understand, making them great areas in which to introduce related signs:

1. Naming things
2. Addressing someone
3. Finding things
4. Knowing something is gone or has run out
5. Asking for more
6. Possessing something

3. INTRODUCE SIGNS IN CONTEXT.

Young children learn best when they can engage their senses in real-world interactions; this is true whether the object is learning to sign, understanding physical properties of the world, or learning to read. Introduce and reinforce signs in meaningful everyday contexts whenever possible. Use the sign before, during, and after an activity.

4. REMEMBER THAT THE DOMINANT HAND MOVES.

In American Sign Language, whenever you perform a sign where one hand moves, it's always your dominant hand (in children's terms, the one you write or draw with) that moves. Any time both hands move, the linguistic rules of ASL dictate that the movement will be symmetrical. If you are right-handed, perform the movement parts of any one-handed sign with your right hand and keep your left hand still; if you are left-handed, perform the movement with your left hand and keep your right hand still. This action will feel most natural to you anyway. Right or left handedness does not establish itself in children until age five or six—indeed, many children go through a stage around age four or five where they use both hands equally as the hemispheres of their brains forge connections with one another. So if your child switches back and forth between dominant hands as he signs, don't worry—this is normal!

5. MAKE EYE CONTACT AND GET IN YOUR CHILD'S LINE OF SIGHT.

Any time your child makes eye contact is an opportunity to sign. With very young children, you may have to actually get down at their level to get in their sight lines before signing.

6. LUXURIATE IN LANGUAGE.

When signing with your child, you have many options! Sign on yourself, on your child, on a puppet, on a picture in a book. Say the words as you sign sometimes, and sometimes sign without speaking. Sometimes take your child's hands and gently help her form the signs. All of these variations will help engage your child in language learning and forge new connections and understandings.

7. KEEP IT POSITIVE AND DON'T GIVE UP.

Even if you are committed to signing with your child, it can be frustrating if your child isn't signing back, or if others in your life don't understand the benefits of signing with children. Just keep going—you *will* see the benefits. Keep your signing interactions with your child positive and fun; signing should never be a chore or a punishment.

8. RESPECT YOUR CHILD'S COMMUNICATION PROCESS.
Whether your child is deaf or hearing, has special needs or doesn't, is six months old or six years old, one of the most important gifts you can give him is the gift of your patient attention when he communicates with you. When you actively listen to your child, without interrupting, you send a powerful message that what he has to say is important. Although this approach sounds simple and obvious, it can be difficult in practice, especially when our children are struggling; after all, we want to help them along in the world. Parents who proactively help each time a child wants to communicate not only deprive that child of the chance to fail—and failure, after all, is life's greatest teacher—but also send the disabling message that *they don't believe their child can succeed without help*. As parents, we can support our children best by providing opportunities for them to practice their skills—and then letting them. Educators Elaine Weitzman and Janice Greenberg, authors of *Learning Language and Loving It* (2002), recommend the "OWL approach":

- **Observe:** Determine what your child is interested in based on nonverbal cues and eye gaze.
- **Wait:** Give the child a chance to initiate communication.
- **Listen:** Pay close attention without interrupting, and respond appropriately.

Weitzman and Greenberg also note that, according to studies, adults tend to give children no more than *one second* to respond before the adult repeats or rephrases. Most children need more processing time than this, so simply waiting is a highly effective communication strategy.

No Magic Pill

Contrary to the way signing with children has been characterized by the media, it is not a magic pill for creating perfectly behaved little angels. Nor is it a fad for creating super-babies. You don't need classes, fancy materials, or flashcards to sign with your child. All you need is you and your willing hands and heart. You don't even need to develop an extensive signing vocabulary in order to see how signing can make your life easier—if you use only one sign with your child, such as MORE, it can short-circuit tantrums and make communication easier. (In the suggested activities that follow, the recommended words to sign are shown in capital letters.)

Of course, once you get started, you're likely to find that this parenting tool is so useful and effective, and so engaging to your child, that you don't want to stop. And why should you? There's a whole language, and a whole world of communication, out there for you and your child to discover together.

Yes, signing and sharing the joy of language with your child take time, energy, and commitment—just like parenting.

chapter 5

Signing at Home

THE ATMOSPHERE IN THE HOME HAS A PROFOUND impact on your child's development, and everyday routines are full of opportunities for interaction, language learning, and bonding. They are also full of opportunities for frustration and miscommunication! Using signs throughout your day helps your child understand and internalize daily routines and develop a sense of security, which is an important foundation for learning. By giving your child tools for communicating easily about daily experiences, you empower him to initiate conversations and take an active role in activities in the home.

Waking Up

Mornings seem to bring out extremes in our temperaments, and kids are no exception. Does your child wake up early, bright-eyed and ready to face the day? Or does she prefer to greet the world a little at a time, easing into contact with other people? Depending on your child's personality—and your own!—mornings can be peaceful or hectic. Often we as adults become so focused on what we need to do in order to get out the door that we forget to do the small things that will help our children start the day with confidence. As with any transitional time, waking up and moving into the more active part of the day can be stressful for babies and young children, so it's important to establish routines and cues that help them feel comfortable with the change. This is especially true as children move into preschool and kindergarten years and are faced with so many new experiences during the school day; the time and attention that you give to your child first thing in the morning can set the tone for the day and allow her to feel more secure during all those new and sometimes stressful activities.

An Active Wake-Up Cue (all ages)

Whatever your child's temperament, an active fingerplay, rhyme, song, or activity that you use consistently can help your child transition to a more active part of the day. You may wish to begin the day with your child's favorite signing rhyme or song, or you may want to list the signs for the things you will do in the morning: potty, brush teeth, get dressed, eat, and so on. If your first stop is the bathroom, think of fun ways to get there—maybe give your child a piggyback ride, or sign an animal and challenge your child to move like that animal.

Why It Works

All of these activities bring an attitude of playfulness to your day and engage your child at his level, while strengthening your relationship and reducing stress for both of you.

Good Morning Song (all ages)

(to the tune of "Good Night Ladies")

GOOD MORNING (*name*),
GOOD MORNING (*name*),
GOOD MORNING (*name*),
It's time to WAKE UP now.

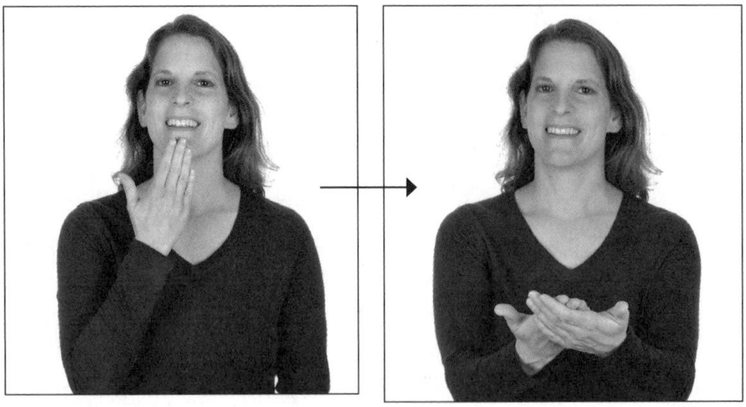

GOOD: The fingertips of one flat hand touch the chin and then move down to rest, palm up, on the other hand, which is flat and facing up.

MORNING: Hold one forearm parallel to the front of your body. Bring the inside elbow of the other arm to the fingertips of the first, with your flat hand held facing up. Move the hand upward to imitate the rising of the sun.

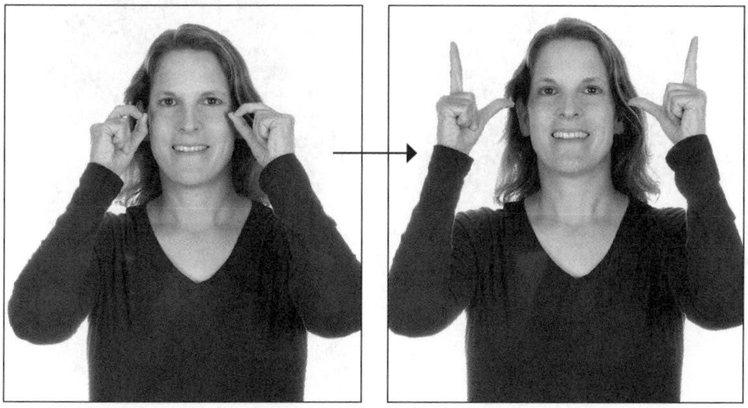

WAKE-UP: Hold the fingertips and thumbs of each hand together at your eyes, to show the eyes closed. Then open them into L-shapes to show the opening of the eyes.

You can incorporate family signs, such as MOMMY, DADDY, and BABY, into this song as well.

If your child is slow to wake, you could even sing the song to different body parts as you tickle them awake ("Good morning, toes . . .").

MOTHER: Tap a 5-handshape on your chin.

FATHER: Tap a 5-handshape on your forehead.

BABY: Hold arms as if rocking a baby.

You can also use this song as a bedtime song by changing the words slightly:

GOOD NIGHT (*name*) . . .
It's time to go to BED.

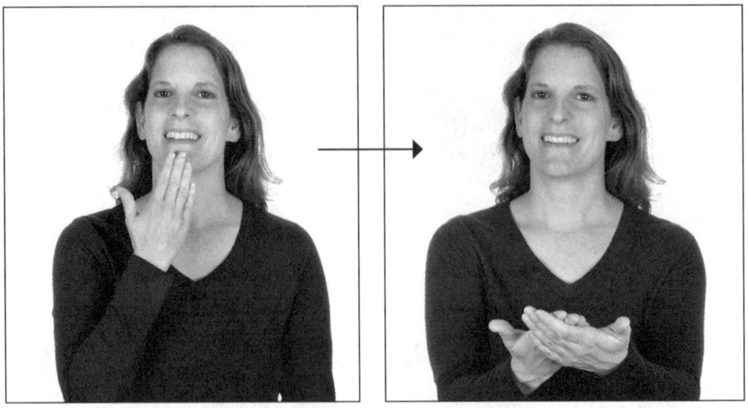

GOOD: The fingertips of one flat hand touch the chin and then move down to rest, palm up, on the other hand, which is flat and facing up.

NIGHT: Hold one forearm parallel to the front of your body. Bend the fingers of the other hand forward and curve them over the first hand to show the sun going down.

BED: Hold both hands flat together against the side of your head as if laying your head on a pillow

Why It Works

Whether or not you think you can sing, your voice is one of the most important sounds in your child's world. Singing during transitional times helps ease fears and increase your child's confidence that everything is okay. (Incidentally, it also forces you to breathe more deeply, which helps control any angry or frustrated reactions you may be experiencing.) Using signs with songs at transitional times also helps distract and engage young children.

READ AND SIGN TOGETHER!

For Babies and Toddlers

Wakey-Wakey by Dawn Apperly. New York: Little, Brown, 1999.
Peekaboo Morning by Rachel Isadora. New York: G. P. Putnam's Sons, 2002.
Wake Up, Me! by Marni McGee. New York: Simon and Schuster, 2002.

For Preschoolers

Giggle-Wiggle Wake-Up! by Nancy White Carlstrom. New York: Knopf, 2003.
Wake-Up Kisses by Pamela Duncan Edwards. New York: HarperCollins, 2002.
Cornelius P. Mud, Are You Ready for School? by Barney Saltzberg. Cambridge, MA: Candlewick, 2007.

Getting Dressed

Getting dressed can be a difficult transitional time for babies, as they have their limbs stuffed into sweaters and pants, or for toddlers and preschoolers who want to do it themselves at their own pace (which is inevitably slower than their parents'). Using sign language rhymes and games before and during the process can help young children shift gears and motivate them to move along.

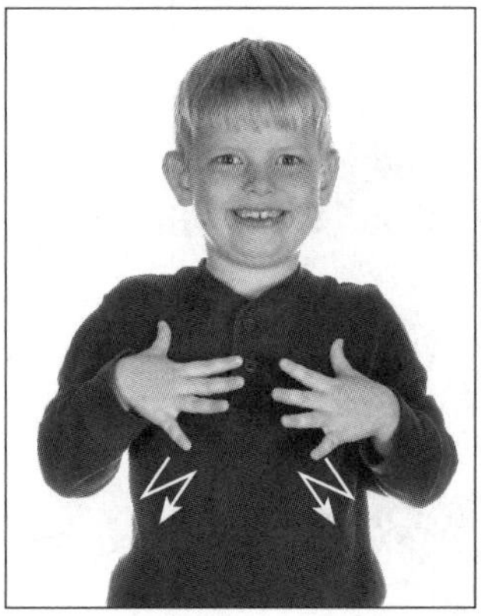

CLOTHES: Brush 5-handshapes downward from chest.

HAT: Tap flat hand on head as if putting on a hat.

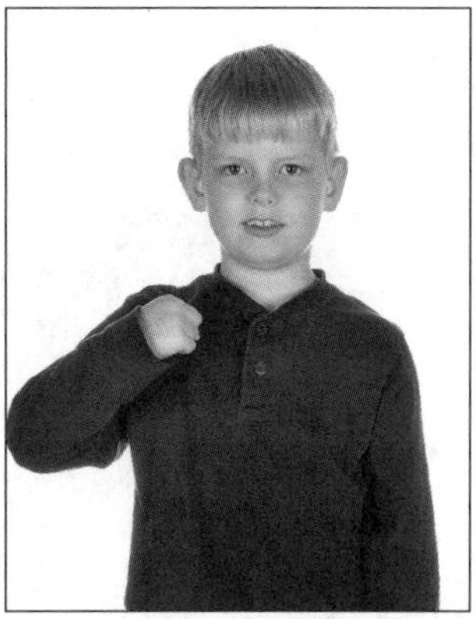

SHIRT: Pinch material of shirt with thumb and index finger.

Wibbety (ages one to six years)

Put on a HAT, wibbety-wat.
Put on a SHIRT, wibbety-wirt.
Put on some PANTS, wibbety-wants . . .

Continue with other items as you help your child get dressed.

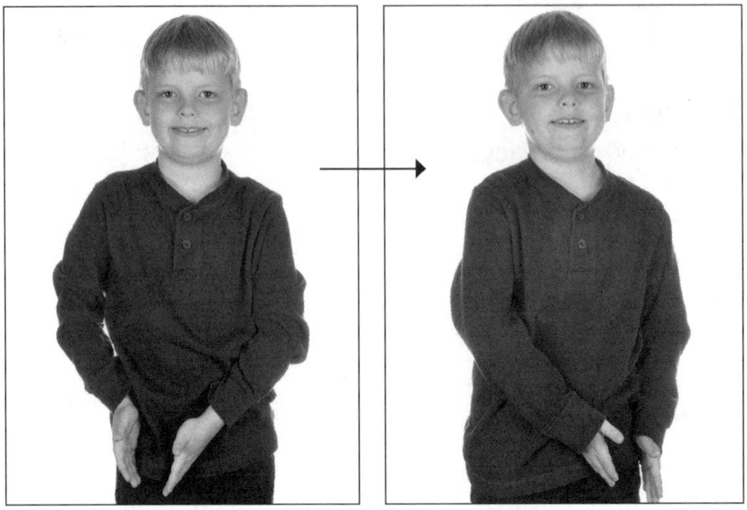

PANTS: Hold flat hands on either side of one leg and then the other.

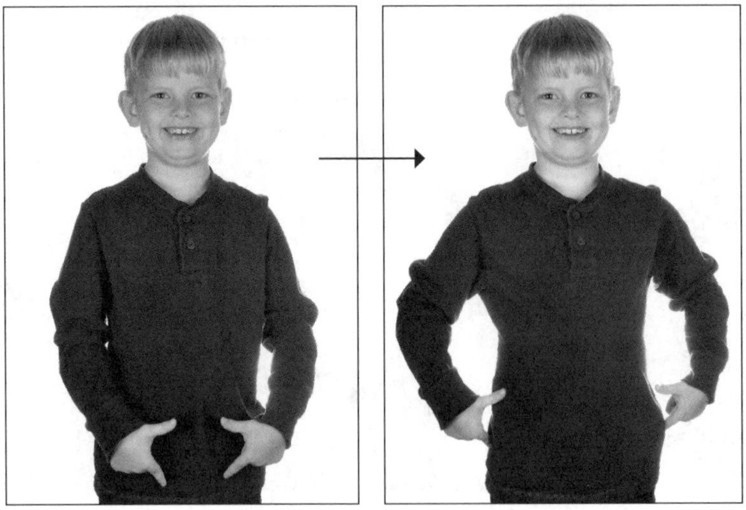

UNDERWEAR: Open thumb and index finger of each hand into a wide C-shape. Hold thumbs at the belly button and then move the open fingers away from each other across the waist and hips to imitate the shape of underwear.

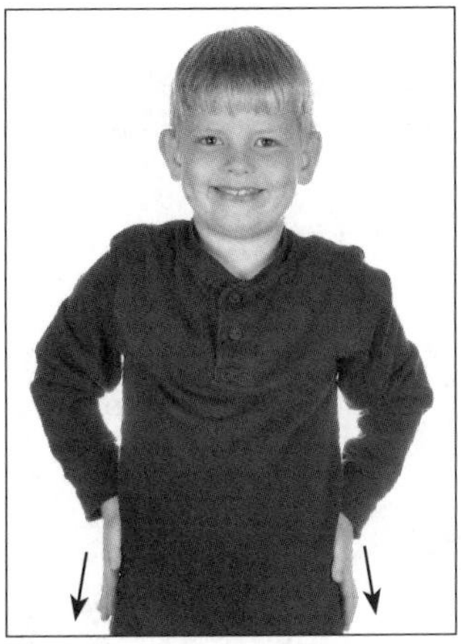

SKIRT: Hold flat hands at waist and move them down and away to show the line of the skirt. (To make this mean DRESS, start the sign above the waist.)

SOCKS: Hold index fingers together pointing down and then move them up and down in alternating motions.

SHOES: Tap two fists together. The fist is the S-handshape, which can help your child remember that shoe starts with the letter s.

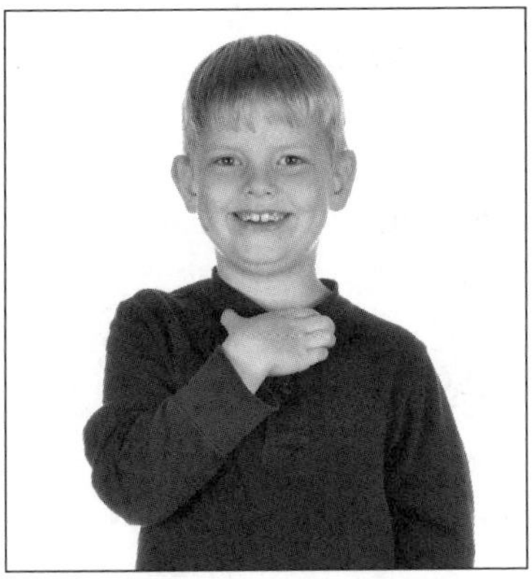

SWEATER: Curve fingers and thumb into a C-shape. Tap C-shape at neck as if making the top of a turtleneck sweater (though this sign applies to any kind of sweater).

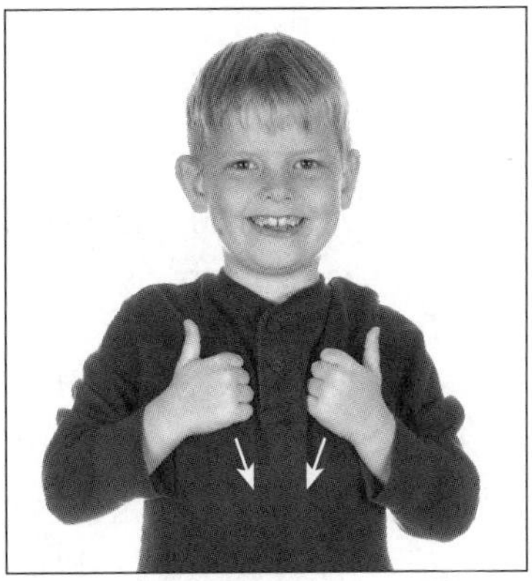

JACKET/COAT: Bend fingers of each hand down to make A-handshapes and then pull the A-handshapes down from the shoulders as if pulling on a jacket.

Why It Works

Babies love the silly sound of the rhyme, and your signs will distract and calm them. The playfulness of the activity assures your child that you are engaged with her even as you are accomplishing your goal of getting your baby dressed.

Toddlers will be engaged by the rhyme, which appeals to their sense of silliness and also helps develop phonemic awareness. If your child is fussy, calmly launching into the rhyme may redirect him without the need for a confrontation. As you say the rhyme with toddlers, pause briefly before you say the clothing item, signing it only. This gives your child a chance to reach for and put on the item, encouraging independence.

Preschoolers will also enjoy the silliness of this activity and may even recite it with you. You can use the same sign-it-first approach with preschoolers as with toddlers, which can encourage a poky preschooler to move along in the getting-dressed process. Or, to make it more of a challenge, try changing the order of the rhyme and letting your child guess the clothing item that rhymes:

Wibbety-wat, put on a . . . HAT!

Initially, you may think, "There's no way I have time for that in my busy morning!" But it takes a lot less time than struggling with an obstinate four-year-old, and you may find your mornings less stressful if you approach them with an attitude of playfulness!

Stinky Socks Song (ages two to six years)

(to the tune of "Twinkle Twinkle Little Star")

STINKY STINKY little SOCKS
I wear you around the clock.
I keep you on my feet all day (*point to feet*)
While I run and jump and play. (*act out the words*)
STINKY STINKY little SOCKS
I wear you around the clock!

STAR: Hold index fingers together pointing up and then move them up and down in alternating motions. Look up at the stars as you make this sign.

SOCKS: Hold index fingers together pointing down and then move them up and down in alternating motions.

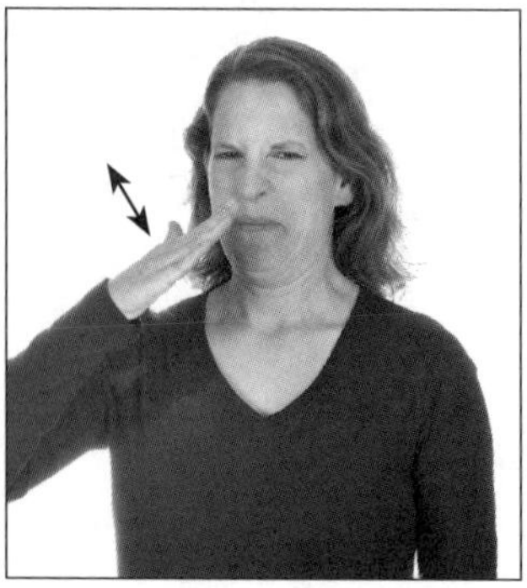

STINKY: Move flat hand back and forth in front of nose as if waving away a stinky smell. Wrinkle your nose as if you smell something bad.

In American Sign Language, the sign SOCK has the same shape and movement as the sign STAR—except that the first points down and the second points up. That's what led me and my son to invent this silly version of an old favorite.

Why It Works

Singing helps children develop phonemic awareness because it clarifies how words are broken down by syllables and emphasizes rhyme. This is an excellent song to sing while wrestling socks onto little feet! Singing new versions of old favorites also encourages creativity and wordplay—ask your preschooler to help you make up new versions of other favorite songs.

READ AND SIGN TOGETHER!

For Babies and Toddlers

Good Morning Sam by Marie-Louise Gay. Toronto, ON: Groundwood Books, 2003.
The First Snowfall by Anne and Harlow Rockwell. New York: Macmillan, 1987.
Max's New Suit by Rosemary Wells. New York: Dial, 1979.

For Preschoolers

Froggy Gets Dressed by Jonathan London. New York: Viking, 1992.
I Can Dress Myself by Birte Müller. New York: NorthSouth, 2007.
Wear a Silly Hat: Sign Language for Clothing by Dawn Babb Prochovnic. Edina, MN: Magic Wagon, 2010.

Diaper and Potty

Stinky Diaper Song (ages birth to three years)

(to the tune of "Frère Jacques")

STINKY DIAPER, STINKY DIAPER
CHANGING time, CHANGING time.
Let's take off the DIRTY one,
Let's put on a CLEAN one.
GLAD you're mine, GLAD you're mine.

Why It Works

Singing just before and during stressful times—such as diaper changes—calms and distracts your baby, making less frustration for you.

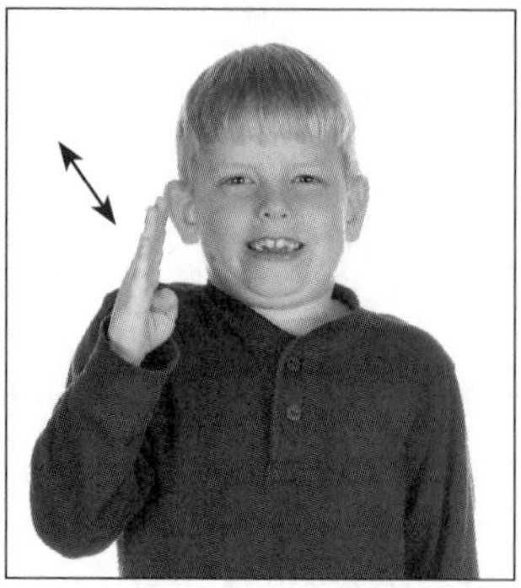

STINKY: Move flat hand back and forth in front of nose as if waving away a stinky smell. Wrinkle your nose as if you smell something bad.

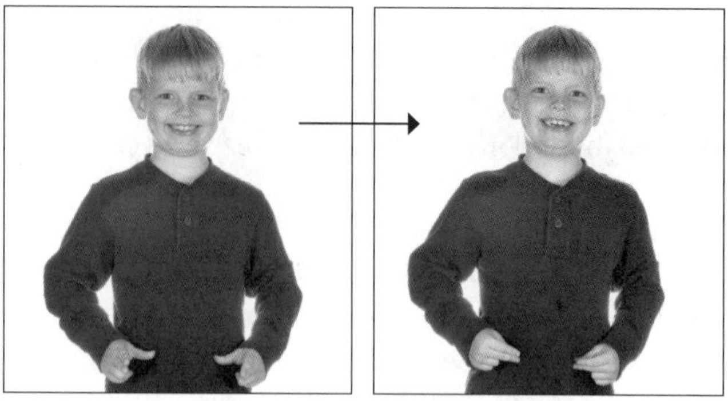

DIAPER: Hold thumbs at waist with index and middle fingers extended. Bring fingers and thumbs together as if fastening a diaper.

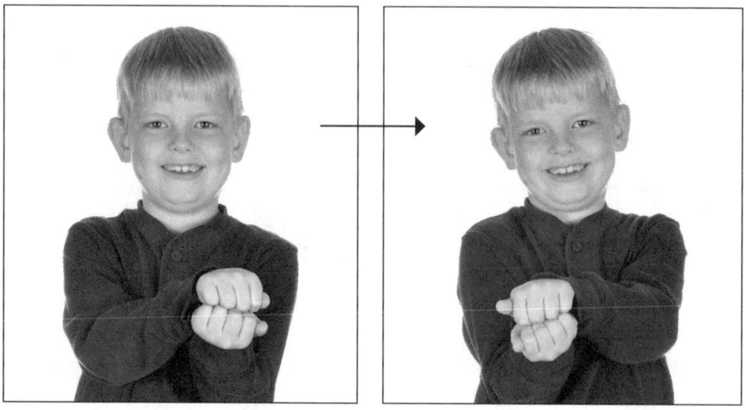

CHANGE: Bend down fingers on each hand and hold tops of fingers together. Twist hands so that one hand ends up below the other.

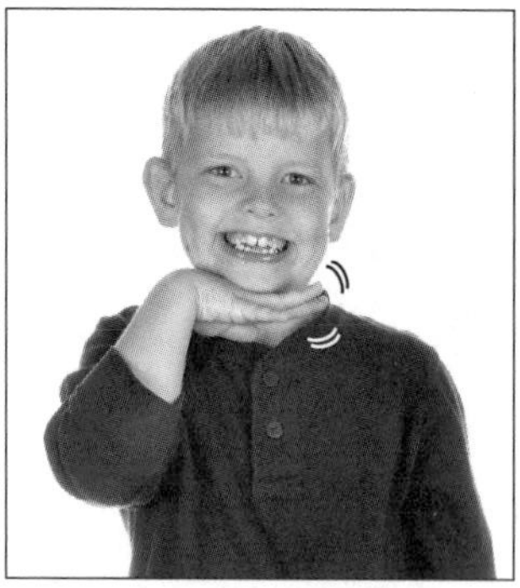

DIRTY: Hold a 5-handshape under your chin and wiggle your fingers. Wrinkle your nose.

CLEAN: Hold a flat hand face-up. Bring the other flat hand, facing down, to the palm of the first hand and then slide it sideways along to the fingers of the first hand.

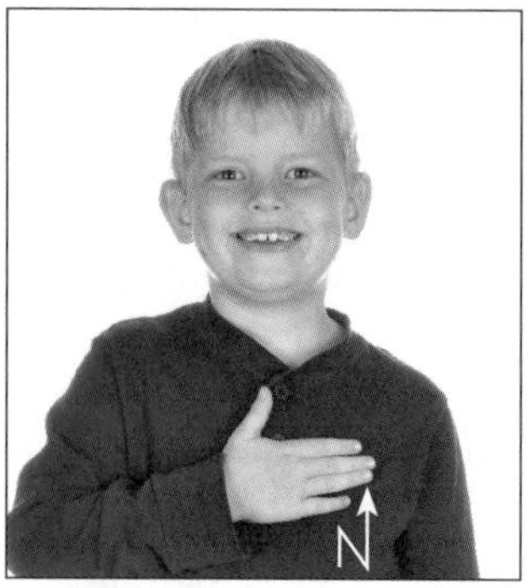

GLAD/HAPPY: Brush a flat hand in an upward motion on your chest. Make sure your facial expression looks happy!

A NOTE ABOUT THE SIGNS

If you look up "change" in an American Sign Language dictionary, you will likely see a sign that uses an X-handshape (a bent index finger). This shape is often difficult for young children to do, so I have chosen a commonly accepted variation that uses the A-handshape—a much simpler shape for little fingers. The five easiest handshapes for young children tend to be the A-, O-, B-, C-, and 5-handshapes. You may notice that your child substitutes one of these shapes for more difficult handshapes even when the correct sign is presented over and over. Don't despair—it just means that her fine motor control is still developing. Accept these variations as your child's production of the sign for now, and keep signing back the correct way—she'll get it eventually!

Potty Doorhanger Craft (ages two to six years)

Directions:

1. Photocopy the craft template from appendix C.
2. Cut out the pieces.
3. Use a pencil to poke a hole in the center of the X on the hand and doorhanger pieces.
4. Place the hand over the doorhanger piece and line up the holes. Use a paper fastener to attach the two pieces.
5. Decorate as desired.
6. Hang the doorhanger on the doorknob and move the hand piece from side to side to sign POTTY!

POTTY: Poke thumb up between your index and middle fingers to make a T-handshape and then shake the "T" from side to side.

DO NOT DISTURB
I am using the
potty!

Why It Works

This simple craft, which actually moves and signs POTTY, is a great way to encourage toddlers to use the potty. Make and decorate this craft together when you begin to potty train your child. Hanging it on the door can provide a key visual cue for potty time and increase children's ownership of the process.

READ AND SIGN TOGETHER!

For Babies and Toddlers

On Your Potty, Little Rabbit by Kathleen Amant. New York: Clavis, 2008.
A Potty for Me by Karen Katz. New York: Little Simon, 2004.
Potty by Leslie Patricelli. Cambridge, MA: Candlewick, 2010.

For Preschoolers

Everyone Poops by Taro Gomi. New York: Kane/Miller, 1993.
Wash Your Hands! by Tony Ross. New York: Kane/Miller, 2000.
Dinosaur vs. the Potty by Bob Shea. New York: Disney Hyperion, 2010.

Mealtime

Mealtime is one of the best times to introduce signs to your child, since she is generally a captive audience and very interested in the subject! For maximum impact, show the food to your child and then show the sign before giving it to her. Repeat each time you mention the food. To encourage your child to use her signs, don't automatically give more food—instead ask, "Do you want MORE CRACKERS?" (signing the words in capital letters). This behavior models the request and helps your child understand how he can use language to ask for more. Wait a moment after you sign the question to give your child a chance to respond, and remember that adults generally don't give children enough time to process and produce language. Count to ten, and if your child doesn't respond, proceed as if she had. Never force a child to sign or speak in order to get the food. Here are more fun activities you can use to emphasize mealtime signs.

Bear Wants More (ages one to six years)

The picture book *Bear Wants More* by Karma Wilson (New York: Margaret K. McElderry, 2003) is a wonderful way to introduce the signs WANT and MORE. Whether by design or by chance, the animals on the cover illustration actually look like they are signing MORE, and the funny rhyming text often repeats the refrain "Bear wants more"! Invite your child to sign this phrase with you throughout the text.

BEAR: Cross open hands over chest with scratching motions.

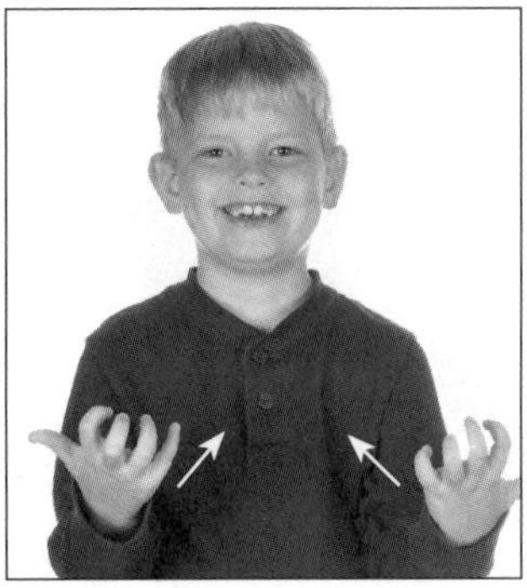

WANT: Hold open hands, facing up, out in front of you. Move them back toward you as you bend your fingers and thumbs.

MORE: Tap gathered fingertips and thumbs of each hand together.

After reading the book, find a favorite teddy to stand in for the bear as you share the following food rhyme. I've used crackers in the example, but you can use any food that you want to emphasize. The signs PLEASE and THANK-YOU are simple enough that you can even make your stuffed bear sign them!

Bear's Food Rhyme (ages one to six years)

BEAR has one CRACKER
And it's YUMMY, that's for sure.
But BEAR is still HUNGRY
So he says, PLEASE, may I have MORE?

When your child gives Bear the food, make Bear sign THANK-YOU. Encourage your child to sign back YOU'RE-WELCOME.

BEAR: Cross open hands over chest with scratching motions.

CRACKER: Tap fist against the elbow of the other arm.

YUMMY: Move flat hand in circles over stomach.

HUNGRY: Hold a C-handshape at the chest, with the palm facing you. Move the C down your chest one time, showing the path of food to the stomach.

PLEASE: Move a flat hand in a circle over your chest.

MORE: Tap gathered fingertips and thumbs of each hand together.

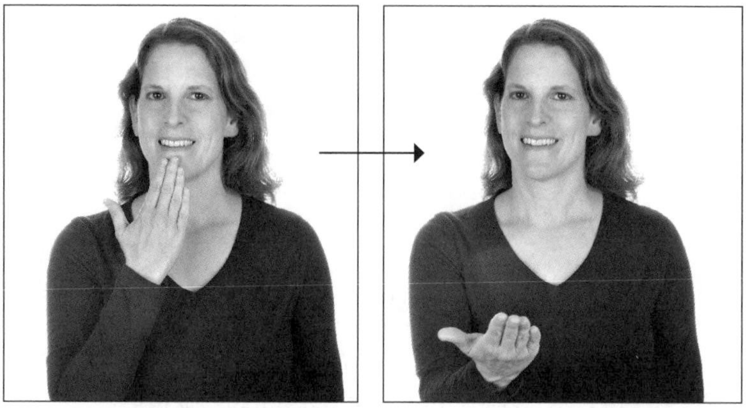

THANK-YOU/YOU'RE-WELCOME: Touch the fingertips of a flat hand to your chin and then move them in the direction of the person you are addressing.

A NOTE ABOUT THE SIGNS

In American Sign Language, there are many ways to politely respond to "thank you," ranging from repeating the sign THANK-YOU to giving a thumbs up. The easiest one to teach your child is the sign THANK-YOU, because it's a sign he already knows. In some books, you may see variations on the sign WELCOME used to mean "you're welcome," but in fact that sign refers to the act of welcoming a person to a place. It's much easier and more linguistically accurate to use the same sign for both "thank you" and "you're welcome."

Why It Works

When you follow up a favorite book with a related rhyme or song, you are helping your child make explicit connections and expand on concepts. By using her own bear and allowing the child to take on the parental role of feeding the bear, you increase interest and allow your child to learn through play. Use real food if possible when playing this game, as the smells and textures of these concrete objects will join the concepts you are emphasizing—that full sensory experience forms new brain connections, and the playful enjoyment of the game releases dopamine, an important neurotransmitter that enhances the ability to focus. Finally, the repetitive, singsong nature of the rhyme allows children to develop a greater understanding of the rhythms of spoken language.

If You're Hungry and You Know It (ages two to six years)

(to the tune of "If You're Happy and You Know It")

If you're HUNGRY and you know it, EAT some FOOD.
If you're HUNGRY and you know it, EAT some FOOD.
If you're HUNGRY and you know it, then your SIGNS will surely show it.
If you're HUNGRY and you know it, EAT some FOOD.
If you're THIRSTY and you know it, take a DRINK . . .
If you WANT MORE and you know it, say MORE PLEASE . . .
If you BURP and you know it, say EXCUSE-ME . . .
If you're FULL and you know it, say ALL-DONE . . .

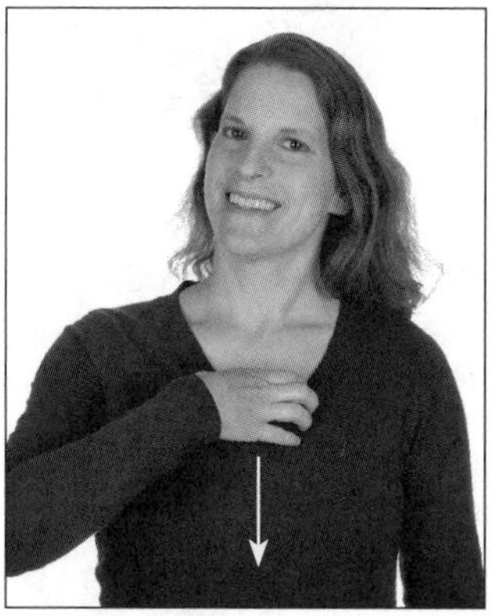

HUNGRY: Hold a C-handshape at the chest, with the palm facing you. Move the C down your chest one time, showing the path of food to the stomach.

EAT/FOOD: Tap gathered fingertips and thumb to mouth.

SIGN: Move index fingers in a circle back toward you.

A NOTE ABOUT THE SIGNS

When signing HUNGRY, be careful to make one downward movement with your hand. If you move the hand downward multiple times, the sign means a different kind of hunger that only applies to grown-ups!

THIRSTY: Drag index finger from chin down throat.

DRINK: Cup hand as if holding a drink and lift it to your lips.

WANT: Hold open hands, facing up, out in front of you. Move them back toward you as you bend your fingers and thumbs.

MORE: Tap gathered fingertips and thumbs of each hand together.

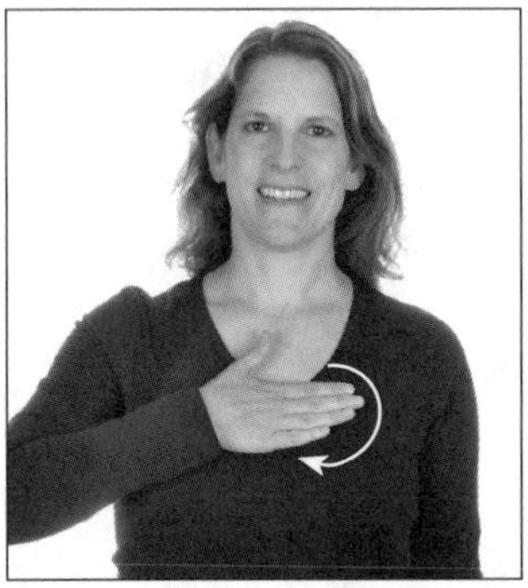

PLEASE: Move a flat hand in a circle over your chest.

EXCUSE-ME: Hold one hand out flat with palm facing up. Bend fingers of the other hand and brush them several times across the palm of the first hand (as if brushing away the offensive thing you did).

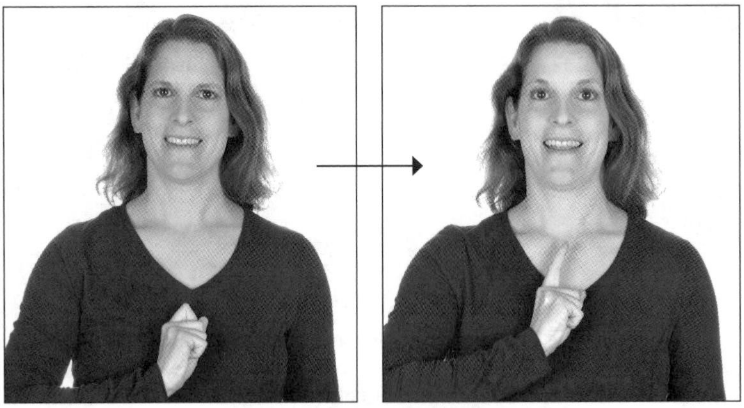

BURP: Hold fist to your chest and then flick index finger upward.

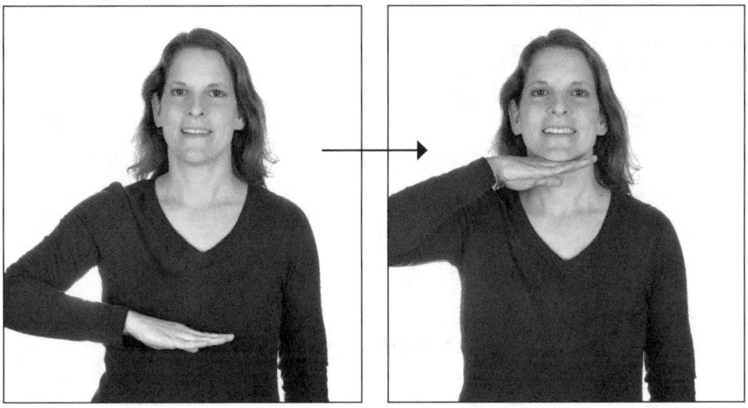

FULL: Hold flat hand, palm facing down, at stomach. Move the hand up to touch chin.

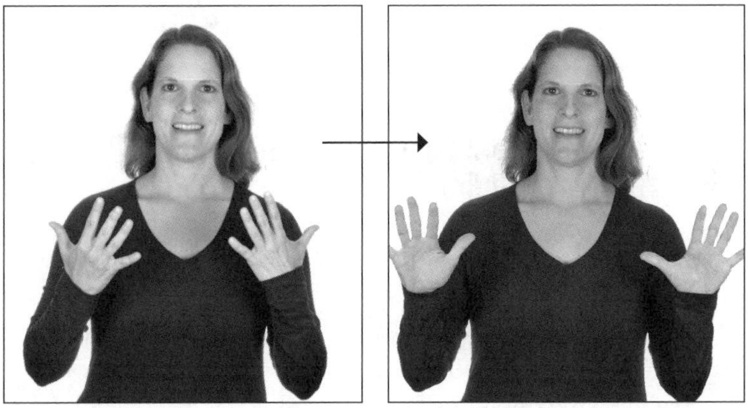

ALL-DONE: Hold flat hands facing you and then turn them to face outward.

Why It Works

This silly song is a fun way to teach and reinforce basic mealtime manners signs. For babies and toddlers, use this song at mealtimes so that they can make concrete connections with the activities discussed. For children ages four and up, you could introduce the songs and signs at any time, but make sure to reinforce them during mealtimes to complete the connections with the actual activities. Once your child knows these basic signs, mealtime can become much more peaceful, as he can ask for more without interrupting someone else's conversation, or even when his mouth is full!

READ AND SIGN TOGETHER!

For Babies and Toddlers

The Very Hungry Caterpillar by Eric Carle. New York: Philomel, 1979.
Early Sign Language: Food Signs. Eugene, OR: Garlic Press, 2002.
Lunch by Denise Fleming. New York: Henry Holt, 1992.

For Preschoolers

Pass the Fritters, Critters by Cheryl Chapman. New York: Four Winds, 1993.
Growing Vegetable Soup by Lois Ehlert. San Diego, CA: Harcourt Brace Jovanovich, 1987.
Feast for Ten by Cathryn Falwell. New York: Clarion, 1993.

Bath Time

Taking a Bath (all ages)

(to the tune of "If You're Happy and You Know It")

We're marching to the BATH, to the BATH.
We're marching to the BATH, to the BATH.
Oh we're going to the tub and we're going to scrub-a-dub.
So we're marching to the BATH, to the BATH.
We're taking off your CLOTHES, off your CLOTHES . . .
We're stepping in the WATER, in the WATER . . .
We're going to use the SOAP, use the SOAP . . .
We SHAMPOO up your hair, SHAMPOO your hair . . .
We rinse you with the WATER, with the WATER . . .
Now the towel DRIES you off, DRIES you off . . .

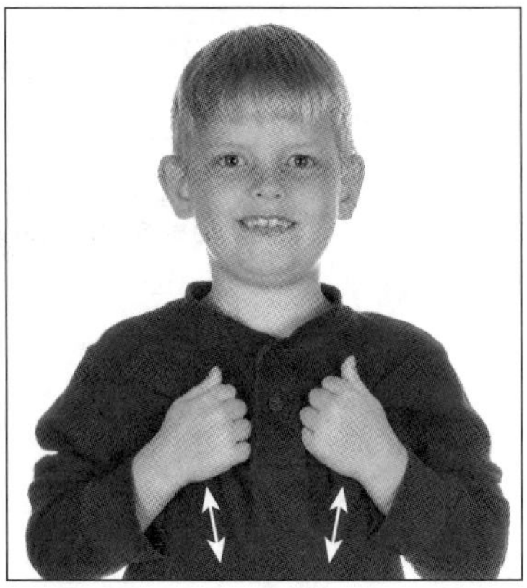

BATH: Bend fingers down to palms. With palms facing you, move hands up and down chest as if bathing.

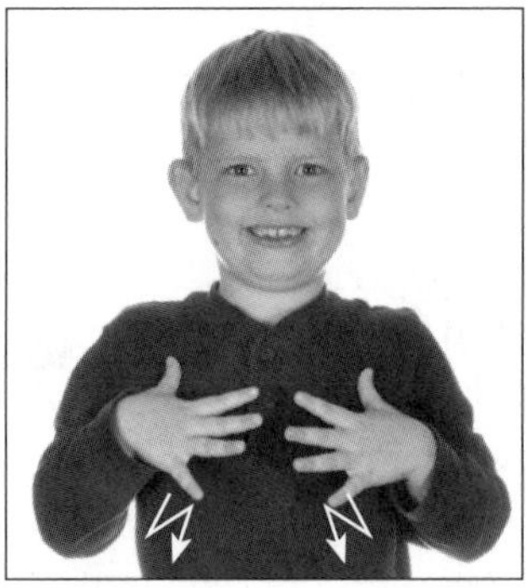

CLOTHES: Brush 5-handshapes downward from chest.

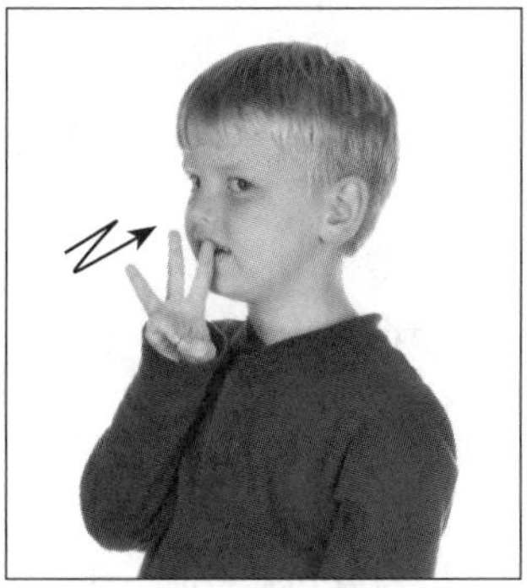

WATER: Hold up first three fingers to make a W. Tap the W to your lips.

SOAP: Hold one hand flat in front of you with palm facing up. Bend fingers of the other hand and rub the fingertips back and forth across the palm of the first hand.

SHAMPOO: Make both hands into claws and rub over hair as if shampooing.

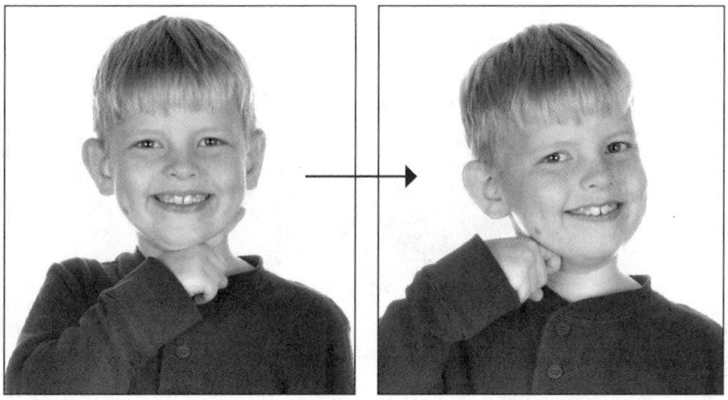

DRY: Extend index finger and place it under your chin. Draw it sideways under your chin, bending your finger as it moves.

Why It Works

Narrating everyday activities like taking a bath helps babies and toddlers process information and match experiences to words. Singing helps children acquire vocabulary as well. You can use this song to cue older children so that they can move along in their bath-time activities themselves. Preschoolers are much more apt to respond to sung and signed cues than to repeated nagging.

Five Bubbles in My Tub (ages one to six years)

(to the tune of "Ten Green Bottles")

ONE little BUBBLE floating in my tub,
ONE little BUBBLE floating in my tub,
And if one more BUBBLE helps me go scrub-a-dub,
There'll be TWO little BUBBLES floating in my tub.

Continue counting bubbles and then ask your child to help you pop the bubbles.

Clap your hands together to "pop" the bubbles, counting down to zero.

BUBBLE: Open and close O-handshapes to represent bubbles.

Why It Works

Babies love to hear your voice. It is the happiest sound in their world. When you combine it with the visual stimulation of signing and the tactile sensations of bathing, this song is a feast for little senses! Toddlers and preschoolers will enjoy participating in the song and signing along. Encourage your child to count with you as you sing the song. With older children, pause before you give the new number at the end of each verse so they have a chance to figure it out and supply it themselves. This opportunity enhances math skills and self-confidence. If you have soap crayons, you and your child could even draw the bubbles on the side of the tub as you count through the song!

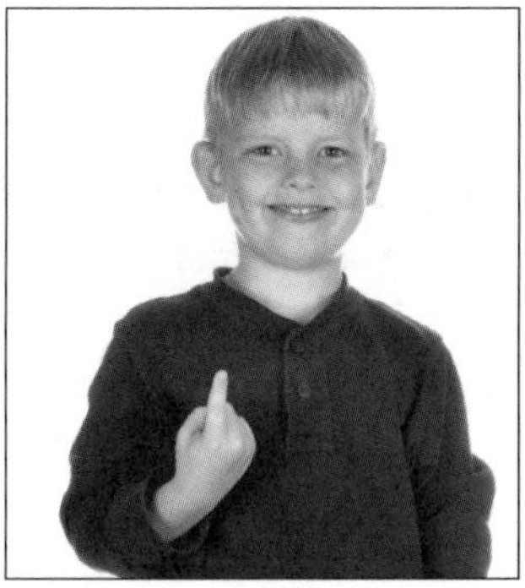

ONE: Hold up index finger with palm facing you.

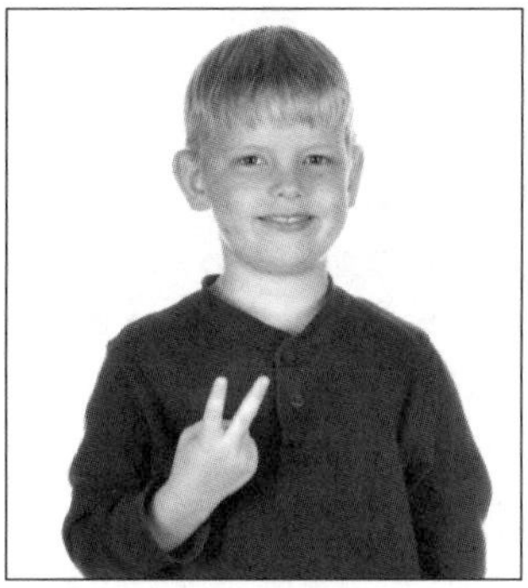

TWO: Hold up index and middle fingers with palm facing you.

THREE: Hold up index and middle fingers and thumb with palm facing you.

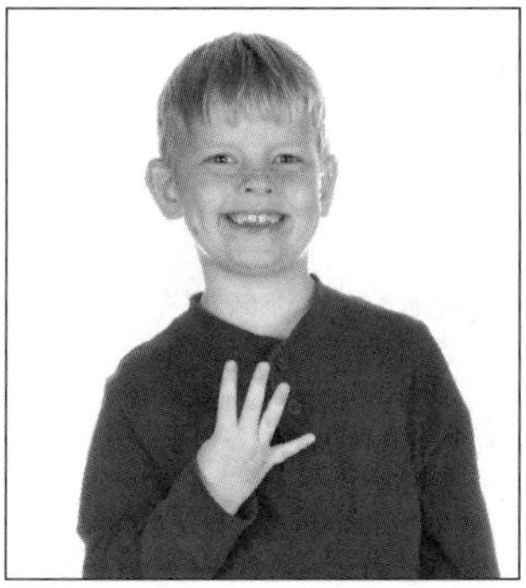

FOUR: Hold up all four fingers with palm facing you.

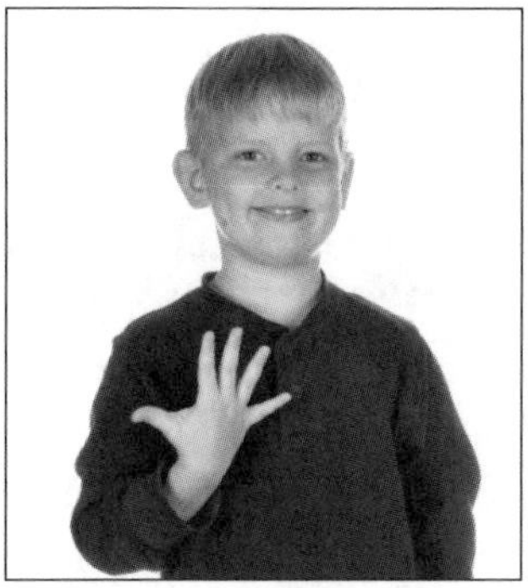

FIVE: Hold up all four fingers and thumb with palm facing you.

ZERO/NONE: Make two O-handshapes and move them away from you.

READ AND SIGN TOGETHER!

For Babies and Toddlers

Bathtime for Biscuit by Alyssa Satin Capucilli. New York: HarperCollins, 1998.

Maisy Takes a Bath by Lucy Cousins. Cambridge, MA: Candlewick, 2000.

Mrs. Wishy-Washy by Joy Cowley. New York: Philomel, 1999.

For Preschoolers

Time to Get Out of the Bath, Shirley by John Burningham. New York: Red Fox, 1978.

King Bidgood's in the Bathtub by Audrey Wood. San Diego, CA: Harcourt Brace Jovanovich, 1985.

Harry the Dirty Dog by Gene Zion. New York: Harper, 1956.

Bedtime

Bedtime can be a difficult transitional time for babies and young children, and if you think about it from their point of view, it's easy to see why. It usually means spending time away from Mom and Dad, in a darkened room, deprived of the toys and fun that mark the day. But sleep is, of course, essential for brain development and energy. You can use sign language in your bedtime routines to help your child settle down and move into a more restful time.

Brush Your Teeth (ages two to six years)

I went to the dentist, and this is what she said:
"Brush your teeth (BRUSH-TEETH) with your hand on your head!"
Brush-a, brush-a, brush-a, brush-a, brush-a, brush-a, brush-a!

I went to the dentist, and she said to me:
"Brush your teeth (BRUSH-TEETH) with your hand on your knee!"
Brush-a, brush-a, brush-a, brush-a, brush-a, brush-a, brush-a!

I went to the dentist, and she said, "Isn't this funny?
Brush your teeth (BRUSH-TEETH) with your hand on your tummy!"
Brush-a, brush-a, brush-a, brush-a, brush-a, brush-a, brush-a!

I went to the dentist, and what do you suppose?
She said, "Brush your teeth (BRUSH-TEETH) with your hand on your nose!"
Brush-a, brush-a, brush-a, brush-a, brush-a, brush-a, brush-a!

I went to the dentist, and she said, "Oh dear!
Brush your teeth (BRUSH-TEETH) with your hand on your ear!"
Brush-a, brush-a, brush-a, brush-a, brush-a, brush-a, brush-a!

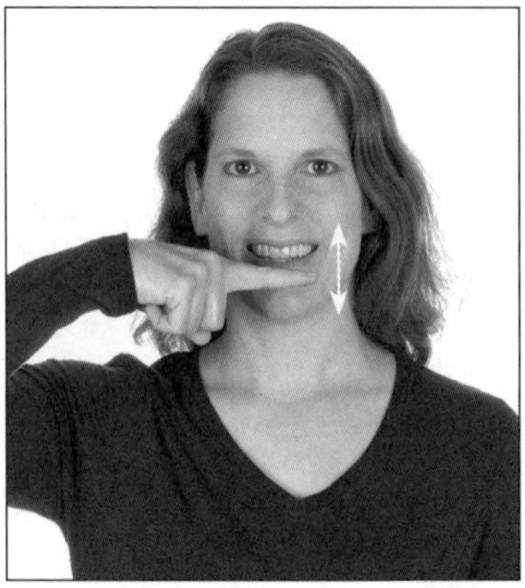

BRUSH-TEETH: Hold index finger horizontally in front of mouth and move it up and down as if brushing teeth.

Why It Works

In my house, toothbrushing time was always a struggle for some reason. Desperate times call for playful measures! I developed this rhyme specifically to get my son moving on brushing his teeth when he didn't want to, and it still works like a charm four years later. Instead of nagging him to brush his teeth, I just launch into this rhyme—he can't stand the thought of missing out on the fun and scrambles to put the toothpaste on his toothbrush! The rhythmic nature of the rhyme appeals to children and helps develop phonemic awareness. For older children, pause before stating where to place the hand to let children guess the rhyme. You can make up infinite variations on this yourself or with your child's help!

Settling Down Rhyme (ages two to six years)

Start by saying the words to this rhyme loudly and rhythmically as you sign it. Repeat the rhyme, making your voice softer and slower each time, until you are only signing it—slowly and gently—with no words.

GOOD NIGHT, STARS.
GOOD NIGHT, TOYS.
GOOD NIGHT, ROOM.
GOOD NIGHT, NOISE.
GOOD NIGHT, MOON up in the sky,
I'll SETTLE down and CLOSE MY EYES.

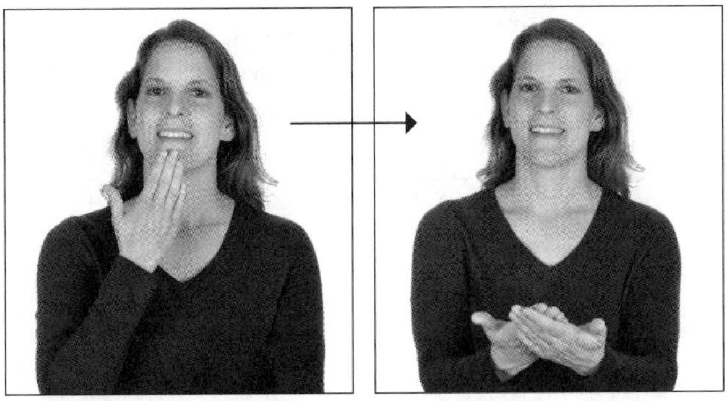

GOOD: The fingertips of one flat hand touch the chin and then move down to rest, palm up, on the other hand, which is flat and facing up.

NIGHT: Hold one forearm parallel to the front of your body. Bend the fingers of the other hand forward and curve them over the first hand to show the sun going down.

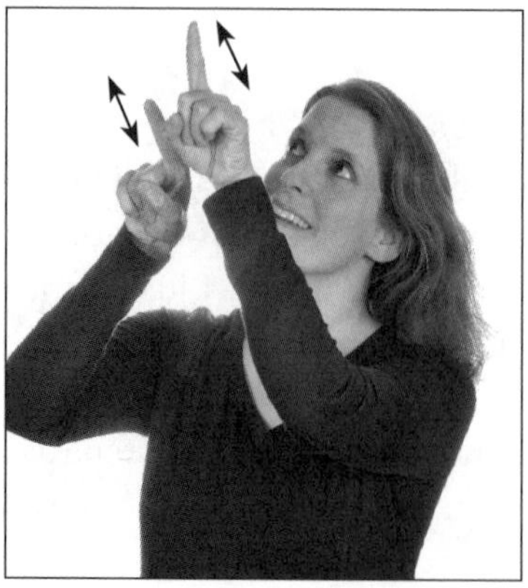

STAR: Hold index fingers together pointing up and then move them up and down in alternating motions. Look up at the stars as you make this sign.

TOY: Poke thumb through the index and middle fingers on each hand to make T-handshapes. Twist the T-handshapes back and forth.

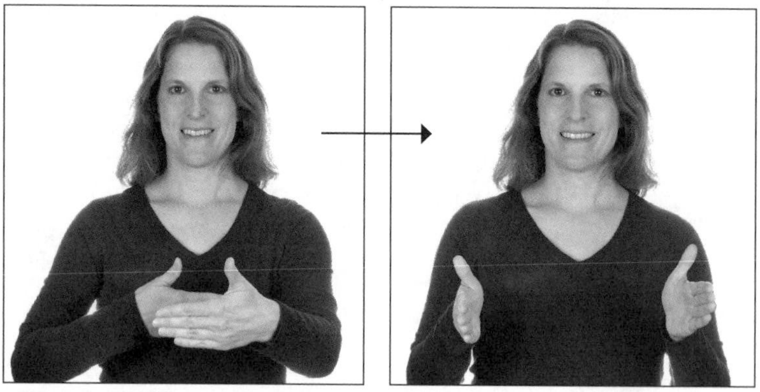

ROOM: Hold flat hands, both palms facing you, in front of your body, with one close to your stomach and one about six inches away. Then move your hands so that the palms face each other. This sign represents the four walls of a room.

NOISE: Hold 5-handshapes, with palms facing down, up by your ears and then shake your hands to show the noise.

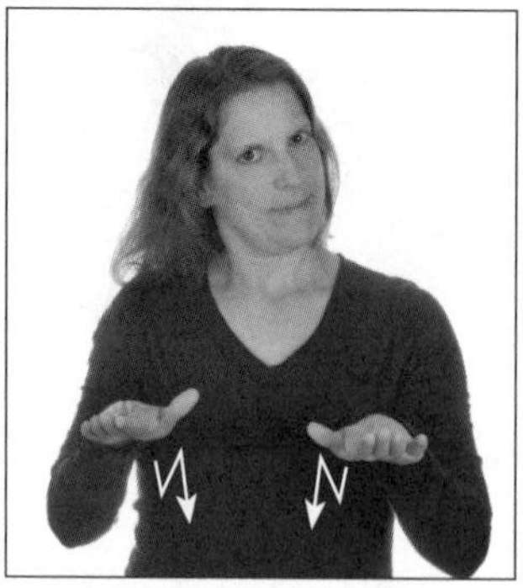

SETTLE: Hold flat hands in front of you with palms facing down and then move them downward.

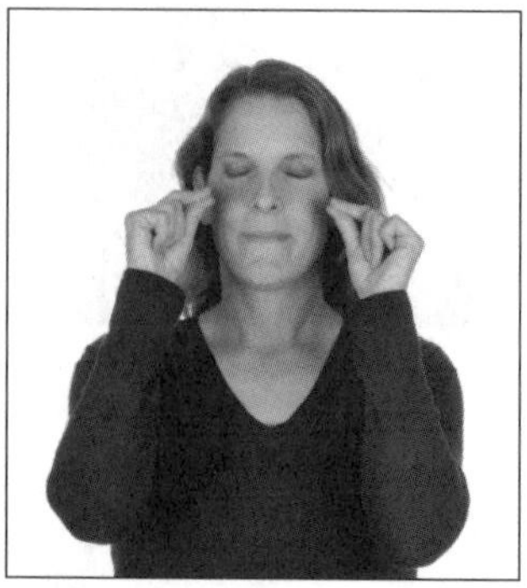

CLOSE-EYES: Bring thumb and index finger of each hand together by your eyes to show the eyes closing.

MOON: Make a crescent moon shape with your thumb and index finger. Hold it up to your eye and then up to the sky.

Why It Works

The noise and rhythm of the rhyme will engage kids, and the gradual lessening of the volume will keep their attention as they try to match your level. And of course, the move from sound to silence gives them an obvious cue to settle down. This activity is also an example of why exposing your child to the use of signs without accompanying words can be beneficial.

ASL Kisses (ages three to six years)

This activity was invented by my son when he was four years old, and it remains one of our favorite bedtime and bonding rituals. It all started when he realized that we could sign KISS together, with each of us pressing one hand in the flat O shape against the other's hand.

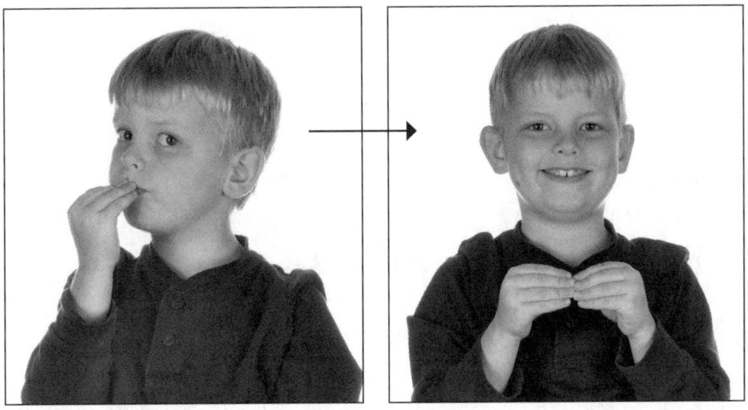

KISS: Bring gathered fingers and thumb to mouth and then touch them to the gathered fingers and thumb of the other hand.

I-LOVE-YOU: Hold up thumb, index finger, and pinky.

I Love You kisses: Press together two I-LOVE-YOU signs.

From there, we invented all kinds of new kisses, and each night, we each pick two ASL kisses to do right before he closes his eyes to go to sleep. (It's also a nice, active parting ritual for day-care drop-off or other good-bye situations.) Some of our favorites are I-LOVE-YOU kisses, ELEPHANT kisses, BIRD kisses, and TREE kisses.

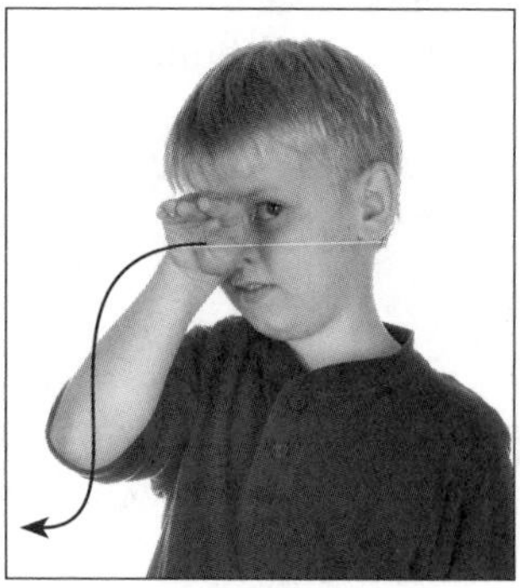

ELEPHANT: Hold a flat hand at the nose and move it down and away from you to show the shape of an elephant's trunk.

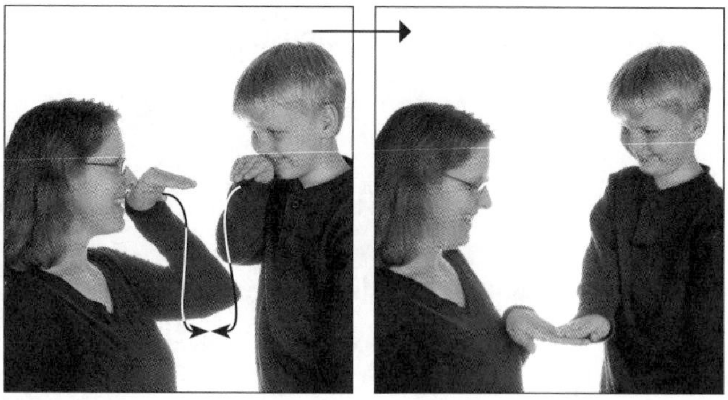

Elephant kisses: Sign ELEPHANT and kiss with the ends of the trunks.

Why It Works

This is a wonderful bonding activity that can help your child funnel sadness or uncertainty into movement and creativity, all the while reaffirming your special connection. You and your child can come up with infinite variations, and encouraging your child to come up with new kisses develops creativity and self-esteem. Playing with language encourages elasticity of thinking. In this case, you are playing with visual language instead of spoken language, but the effect on your child's brain development is the same.

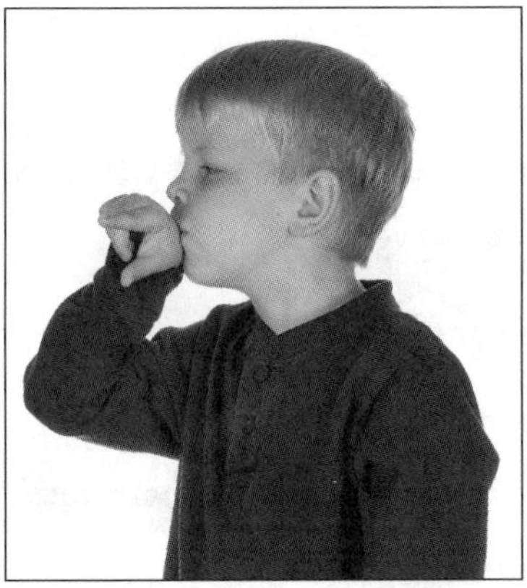

BIRD: With palm facing away from you and hand held in front of mouth, open and close your index finger and thumb to represent a beak.

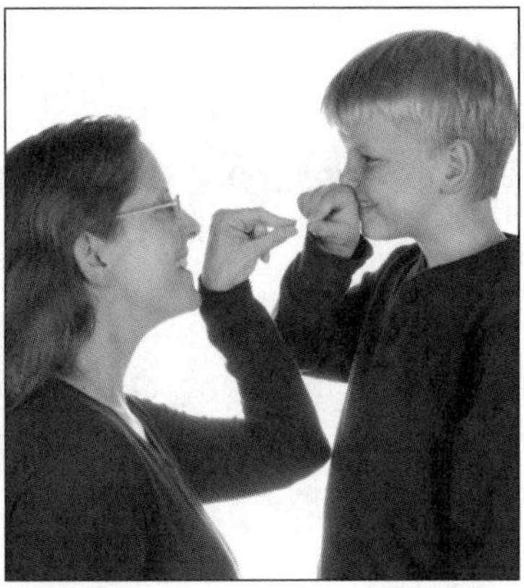

Bird kisses: Sign BIRD and kiss with the beaks.

TREE: Shake a 5-handshape to represent a tree moving in the wind.

Tree kisses: Sign TREE and make the two trees bend toward each other and kiss.

READ AND SIGN TOGETHER!

For Babies and Toddlers

Goodnight Moon by Margaret Wise Brown. New York: Harper and Row, 1947.
Time for Bed by Mem Fox. New York: Gulliver, 1993.
Say Goodnight by Helen Oxenbury. New York: Little Simon, 1987.

For Preschoolers

Sheep Don't Count Sheep by Margaret Wise Brown. New York: Margaret K. McElderry Books, 2003.
Hush! A Thai Lullaby by Minfong Ho. New York: Orchard, 1996.
Sleep, Sleep, Sleep: A Lullaby for Little Ones around the World by Nancy Van Laan. New York: Little, Brown, 1995.

Family

Who Loves You, Baby? Surprise Frame and Rhyme

(ages six months to two years)

Cut a piece of fabric the same size as a picture frame. Glue or tape the fabric over the picture frame, attaching it only at the top. Place a picture of a family member or pet inside the frame. Then say the rhyme and reveal the special person or animal. Keep multiple pictures that will fit into the frame so you can switch them out.

Who Loves You, Baby?

(to the tune of "Skip to My Lou")

Hey there, BABY, who LOVES you?
Who's that playing peek-a-boo?
It's somebody you LOVE too.
(*Name*), that is who LOVES you!

BABY: Hold arms as if rocking a baby.

LOVE: Cross fists over chest as if giving yourself a hug.

Why It Works

Babies are naturally drawn to faces. Using photos of familiar loved ones increases a child's engagement in and enjoyment of the activity and helps her understand both spoken and signed language in context. Every child loves to hear and see assurances that she is loved and cared for. Emotional health and a sense of security are important prerequisites for intellectual skills.

A NOTE ABOUT THE SIGNS

American Sign Language has linguistic and cultural rules regarding name signs. Unlike in American hearing society, name signs are actually given to an individual by the Deaf community and linguistically belong to that community, not the individual. In ASL, it's very rare to use a name sign when addressing someone—after all, in a visual language, a person knows you are addressing him or her because you are making eye contact! Name signs are generally used when referring to someone in the third person, particularly if that person is not present.

For your purposes, you will most likely be using name signs for brothers, sisters, and friends. Here is the easiest way to come up with appropriate name signs:

1. Find the sign for the first letter of the person's name on page 108.

2. If the person is a girl, sign the letter at the chin (where the female signs are located). If the person is a boy, sign the letter at the forehead (where the male signs are located).

3. If you have more than one person of the same gender whose names start with the same letter, choose from these locations for the others:
    - at the chest
    - shake the letter in the neutral area in front of the body
    - sign the letter at the forehead and then at the chin

The People in the Family (ages two to six years)

(to the tune of "The Wheels on the Bus")

The BABY in the FAMILY says "wah-wah-wah," "wah-wah-wah,"
"wah-wah-wah,"
The BABY in the FAMILY says "wah-wah-wah," all day long.
The SISTER in the FAMILY says "ha-ha-ha" . . .
The BROTHER in the FAMILY says, "Let's all play" . . .
The DADDY in the FAMILY says, "Come on home" . . .
The MOMMY in the FAMILY says, "I love you" . . .
The GRANDMOTHER in the FAMILY says, "Let's read a book" . . .
The GRANDFATHER in the FAMILY says, "Let's take a walk" . . .
The AUNT in the FAMILY says, "Give me a kiss" . . .
The UNCLE in the FAMILY says, "Give me a hug" . . .
The COUSINS in the FAMILY say, "Let's go outside" . . .

Adapt the words of the song so that the family members say things that your child's relatives might say! The more closely the song ties to your child's real-life experiences, the more it will engage and benefit him.

BABY: Hold arms as if rocking a baby.

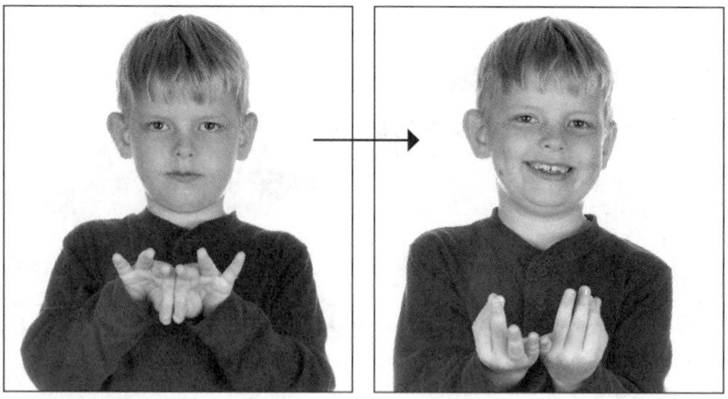

FAMILY: Hold the thumb and index finger of each hand together, with the other fingers up, to make an F-handshape. Place the two F-handshapes next to each other with your palms facing away from you. Then move the F-handshapes forward in a circle so that the pinky sides of your hands meet in the front.

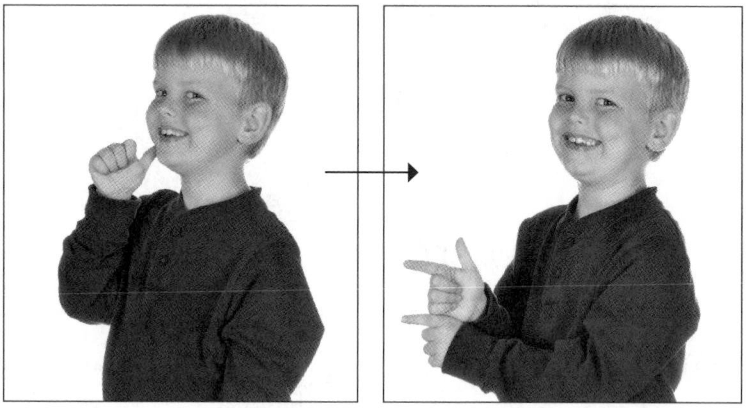

SISTER: Hold thumb to chin and then stack hands in front of you with index fingers pointing forward.

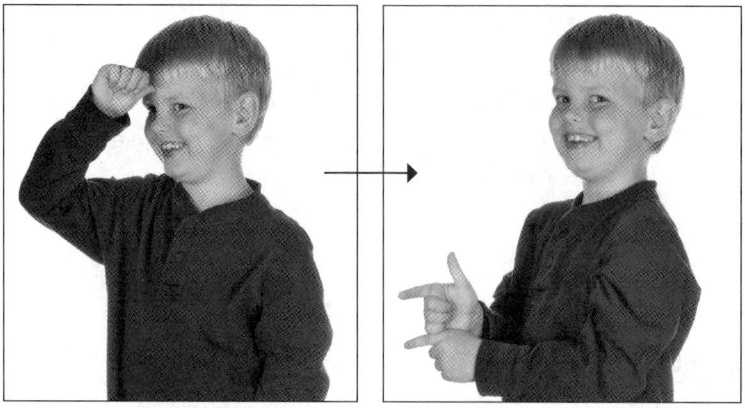

BROTHER: Hold thumb to forehead and then stack hands in front of you with index fingers pointing forward.

FATHER: Tap a 5-handshape on your forehead.

MOTHER: Tap a 5-handshape on your chin.

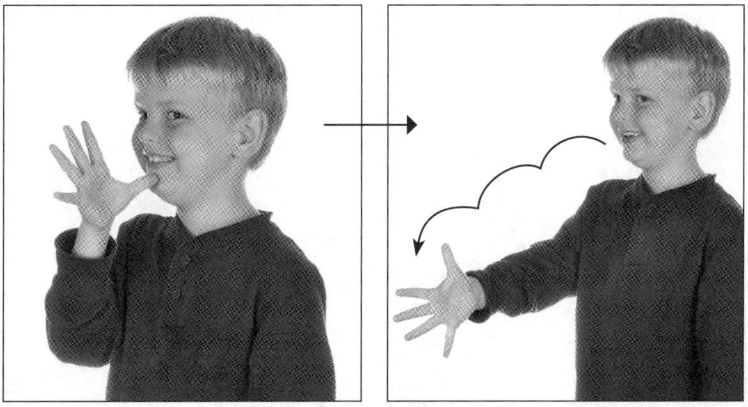

GRANDMOTHER: Move a 5-handshape away from your chin in a bouncing motion.

GRANDFATHER: Move a 5-handshape away from your forehead in a bouncing motion.

AUNT: Make an A-handshape by bending your fingertips over to touch your palm and keeping your thumb out. Move the A-handshape in a circular motion near your chin.

UNCLE: Make a U-handshape by holding up your index and middle fingers pressed close together. Move the U-handshape in a circular motion near your forehead.

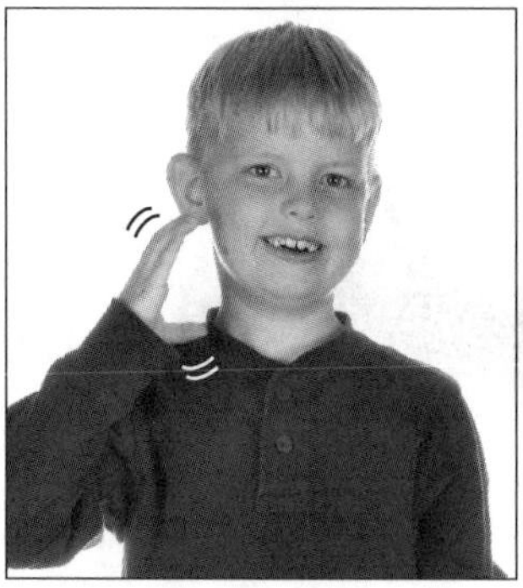

COUSIN (FEMALE): Shake a C-handshape by your chin.

COUSIN (MALE): Shake a C-handshape by your forehead.

COUSINS (MALE AND FEMALE): Shake a C-handshape by your cheek.

Why It Works

Combining songs with sign language is a feast for the senses—and the senses are the primary vehicles that young children use to learn about their world. Singing helps children internalize important concepts about phonology, as it emphasizes separate syllables of the words in a way that everyday speech does not. At the same time, signing emphasizes meaning and helps children understand the song and participate in it kinesthetically. This is why it is especially important to use conceptually accurate signs that focus on meaning, instead of worrying about specific English words. For example, the word *running* has many meanings in English, from "running in a race" to "running for office" to "my nose is running." These would all be signed differently in ASL, because they mean completely different things!

Hug Card Craft (ages three to six years)

Directions:

1. Photocopy the template from appendix C.
2. Cut out the pieces along the solid lines.
3. Glue the circle on the top of the card. Glue the two small circles to the ends of the arms.
4. Decorate the face and body and glue yarn on top for hair.
5. Write a special message along the inside of the arms. For a special surprise, write the beginning of the message on the outside of the arms and the end of it on the inside.
6. Fold up the arms on the dotted lines. This creates the sign LOVE.
7. Give the card to someone you love!

LOVE/HUG: Cross fists over chest as if giving yourself a hug.

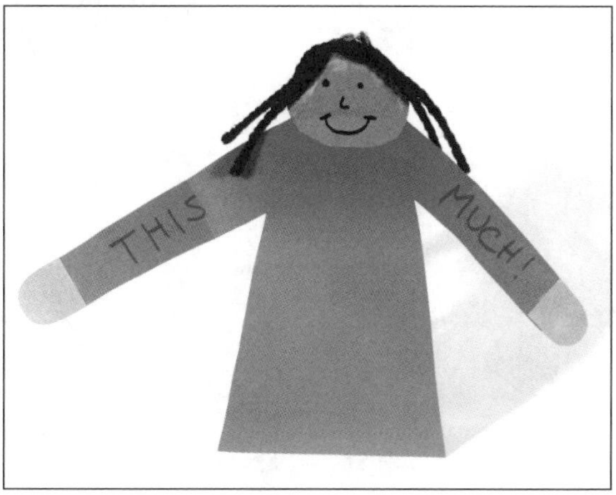

Why It Works

This craft is simple enough for toddlers to decorate (with help) and provides a nice challenge for older children ready to exercise their fine motor skills through cutting, drawing, and writing. With the card's visual demonstration of the sign LOVE, no giver or recipient is likely to forget the sign! Allowing children to decorate the card in any way they like encourages creativity and elasticity of thinking.

READ AND SIGN TOGETHER!

For Babies and Toddlers

Spot Visits His Grandparents by Eric Hill. New York: Putnam, 1996.
Mommy Hugs by Karen Katz. New York: Margaret K. McElderry Books, 2006.
Family by Helen Oxenbury. New York: Simon and Schuster, 1981.

For Preschoolers

My Family Is Forever by Nancy Carlson. New York: Penguin, 2004.
Peter's Chair by Ezra Jack Keats. New York: Viking, 1967.
Families Are Different by Nina Pellegrini. New York: Holiday House, 1991.

chapter 6

Staying Safe and Having Fun

IN THIS CHAPTER, WE FOLLOW THE CHILD'S EXPANDing world as she moves into playing with others both at home and away and begins to see how specific behaviors lead to positive or negative consequences. Because signing offers a kinesthetic and tactile experience of language, it helps young children develop an understanding of intangible concepts such as feelings and behavior.

Safety and Health

Do We Touch It? (ages two to six years)

Assemble a variety of objects, some of which are safe to touch, some of which are unsafe to touch. (Be sure to keep the latter group out of your child's reach! If the idea makes you nervous, you can use pictures instead, but real objects will be more effective.) Here are some ideas for the objects:

Safe to touch: teddy bear, children's book, rubber duck, blanket, puppet
Unsafe to touch: candle, scissors, knife, hot cup of coffee, oven

TOUCH: Touch middle fingertip of one hand to the back of the other hand.

DON'T-TOUCH: Touch middle fingertip of one hand sharply to the back of the other hand while shaking your head.

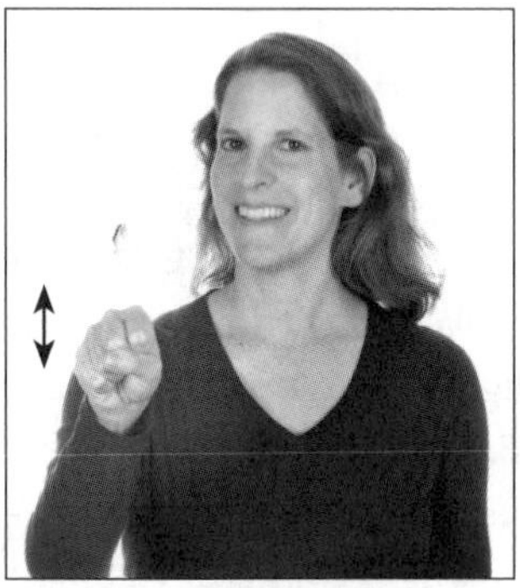

YES: Move fist up and down to represent a head nodding.

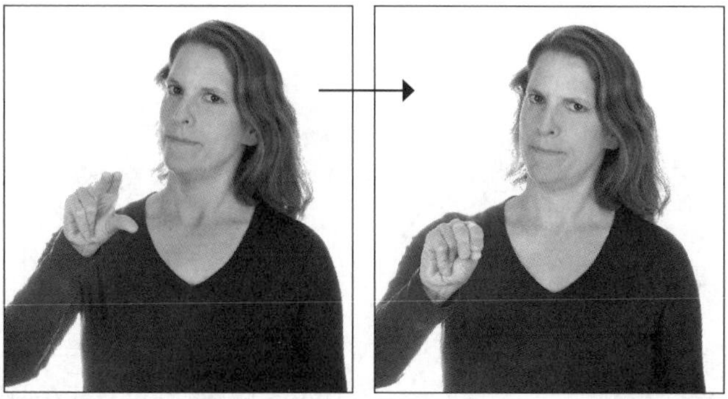

NO: Bring first two fingers and thumb together while shaking your head.

Show your child an object. Introduce the signs TOUCH, DON'T-TOUCH, YES, and NO as follows:

"Here's a very sharp knife. Should I TOUCH it? Is it safe? NO, we DON'T-TOUCH this! We could get hurt!"

"Look, here's a soft teddy bear. Do you think I should TOUCH the teddy bear? YES, we can TOUCH the teddy! You TOUCH it too!"

Make sure to use lots of animation in your signs and your voice to emphasize the meaning of the signs. Repeat the game with different objects. Once you have introduced and reinforced the signs with this activity, use the signs in everyday situations to help your child understand what is and is not safe to touch.

Why It Works

Young children learn best in context, so the best language and literacy connections happen during everyday interactions with real objects. When you conduct this interactive game with your child, you are inviting her to take part in developing understanding through manipulating real-world objects. Additionally, the suspense created by the idea that you might actually touch the forbidden objects stimulates engagement. Setting up the game so that your child can show you what she already knows reinforces self-control, self-esteem, and self-expression and emphasizes how much you want to hear what she has to say.

A NOTE ABOUT THE SIGNS

The only difference between the signs TOUCH and DON'T-TOUCH is in the movement of your head and your facial expression, so it's important to make those things very clear! In fact, over 80 percent of the meaning in American Sign Language is conveyed by nonmanual signals (facial expression, body movement, and speed and sharpness of signing), not by what the hands are doing!

Patience Freeze Dance (ages one to six years)

This fun activity encourages listening and self-control. Explain that you are going to listen to some music, and when the music is playing, the child should DANCE. But when the music stops, he should freeze and be PATIENT or WAIT. Play music and encourage your child to dance along by signing DANCE. Periodically pause the music and then sign PATIENT or WAIT until it resumes again. You can also use ready-made freeze dances that have the pauses built in, such as these:

"Rock and Roll Freeze Dance" from *"So Big": Activity Songs for Little Ones* by Hap Palmer (Topanga, CA: Hap-Pal Music, 1994).

"The Freeze" from *We All Live Together*, volume 2, by Greg and Steve (Los Angeles: Youngheart, 1978).

"Can't Wait to Celebrate" from *Jim Gill's Irrational Anthem* by Jim Gill (Oak Park, IL: Jim Gill Music, 2001).

For older kids, follow up with a "listening with your eyes" freeze dance. Instruct your child to watch you. Without speaking, sign DANCE when you want your child to dance and PATIENT or WAIT when you want her to stop. Then let your child have a chance to be the leader!

DANCE: Hold palm of one hand facing up. Hold index and middle fingers of the other hand in an upside-down V-handshape over the palm. Move the fingers side to side to represent legs dancing.

PATIENT: Fold fingers down to palm. Press back of thumb to mouth in a downward motion.

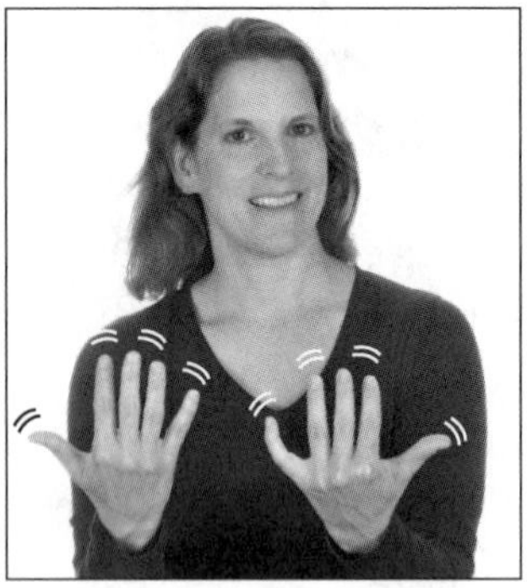

WAIT: Hold both hands in front of you with palms facing you. Wiggle the fingers.

Why It Works

This is a fun and active way to introduce and reinforce the signs PATIENT or WAIT, or both, which you can then use in everyday situations to cue your child. Introducing your child to the idea of signing without speaking allows you to give behavior cues to your child silently when in public or in quiet places like church or a theater. You may even find that your child uses these signs as an outward cue to himself as an aid to self-control.

A NOTE ABOUT THE SIGNS

For some reason, the sign PATIENT tends to be more effective with children than the sign WAIT—perhaps because PATIENT incorporates both the waiting and the way you want someone to behave while doing it. After all, it's possible to WAIT impatiently!

Five Little Monkeys (ages one to six years)

(traditional)

FIVE little MONKEYS JUMPING on the BED.
ONE FELL OFF and BUMPED his head.
MAMA CALLED the DOCTOR and the DOCTOR SAID,
"No more [ALL-DONE] MONKEYS JUMPING on the BED."

Repeat, counting down to zero.

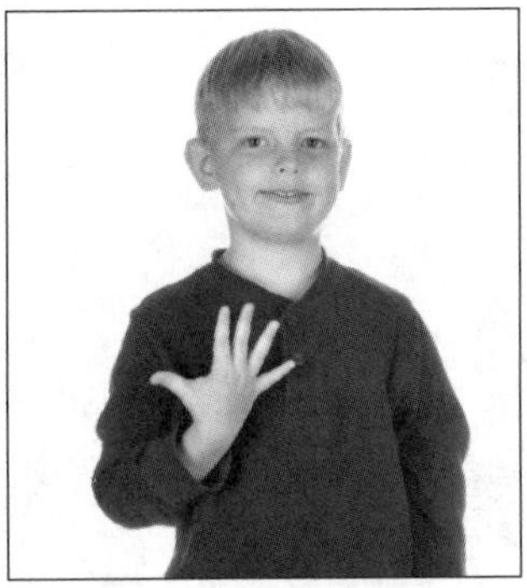

FIVE: Hold up all four fingers and thumb with palm facing you.

MONKEY: Hold clawed hands at waist and scratch like a monkey.

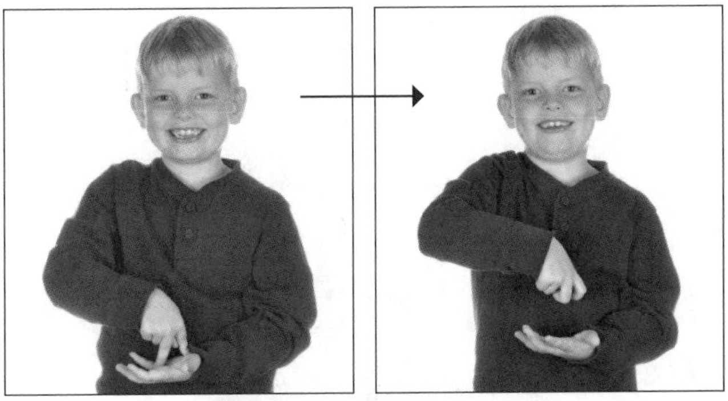

JUMP: Hold one hand out with palm facing up. Make an upside-down V shape with the index and middle fingers of the other hand and make it jump up and down on the palm.

BED: Hold both hands flat together against the side of your head as if laying your head on a pillow.

ONE: Hold up index finger with palm facing you.

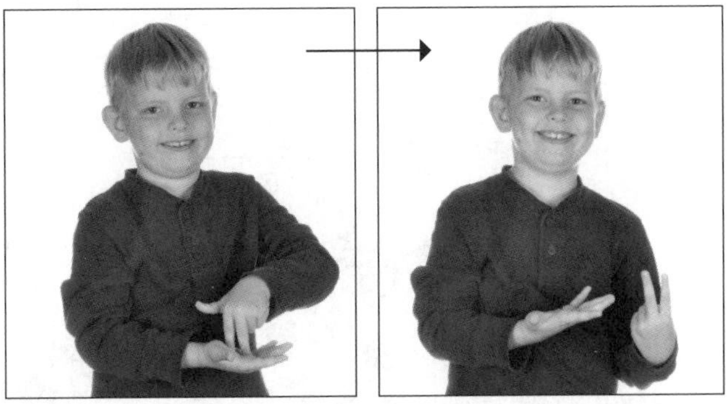

FALL-OFF: Hold one hand out with palm facing up. Make an upside-down V-handshape with the index and middle fingers of the other hand and make it fall off of the palm.

BUMP-HEAD: Bring palm to forehead.

MOTHER: Tap a 5-handshape on your chin.

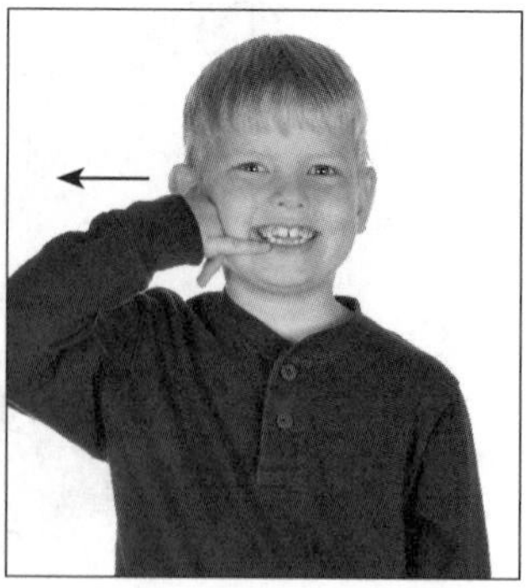

CALL: Put up thumb and pinky to make a Y-handshape. Hold the Y at your ear and then move it outward.

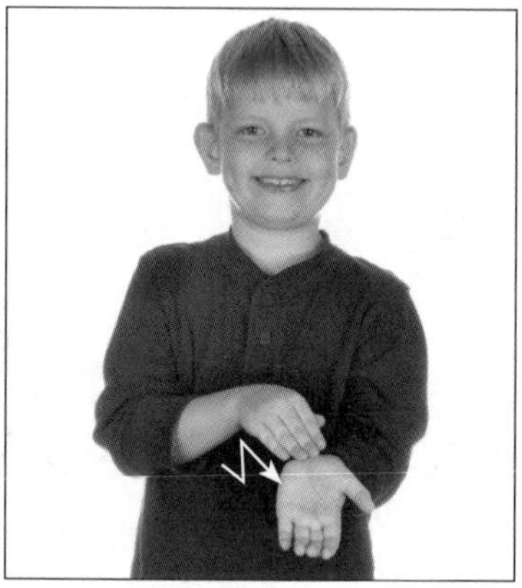

DOCTOR: Bring the bent fingers of one hand to the opposite wrist, as if checking a pulse.

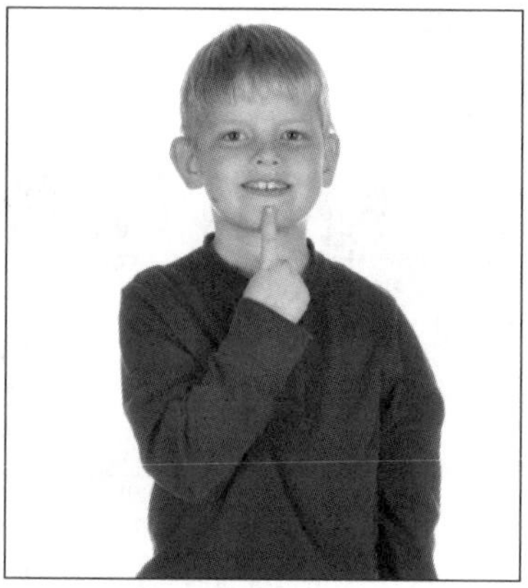

SAY: Point to mouth.

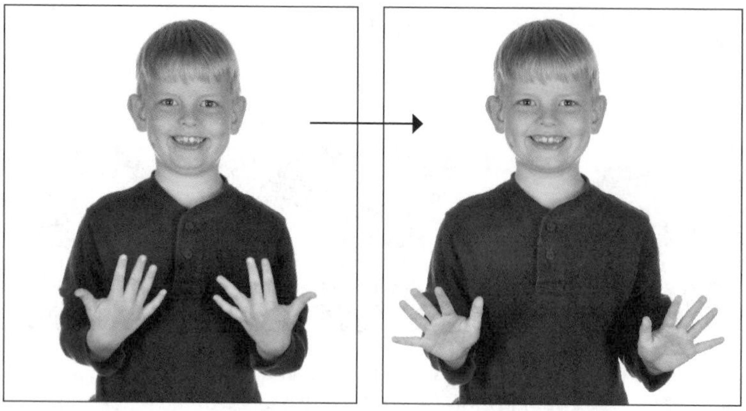

ALL-DONE: Hold flat hands facing you and then turn them to face outward.

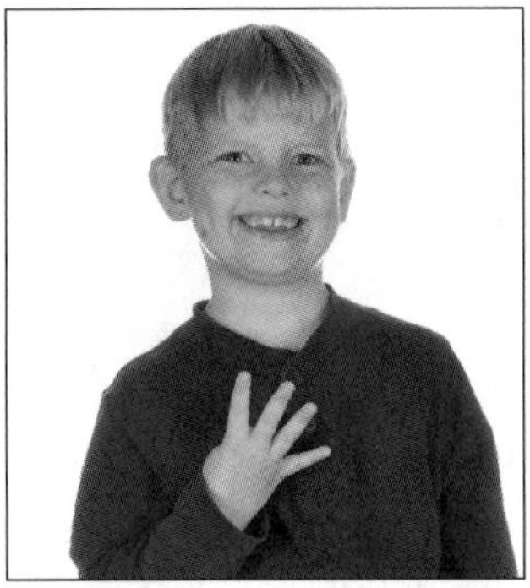

FOUR: Hold up all four fingers with palm facing you.

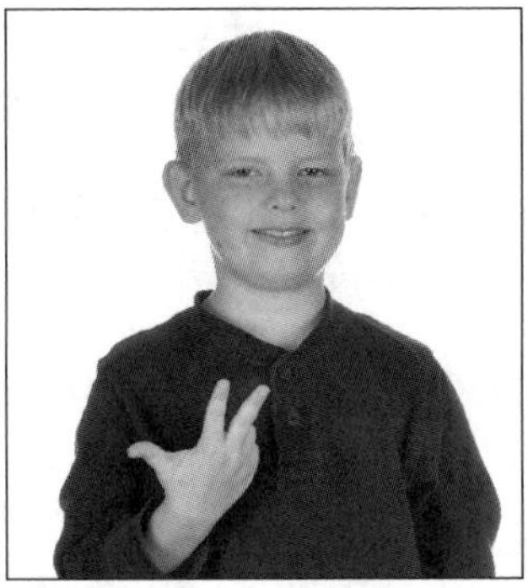

THREE: Hold up index and middle fingers and thumb with palm facing you.

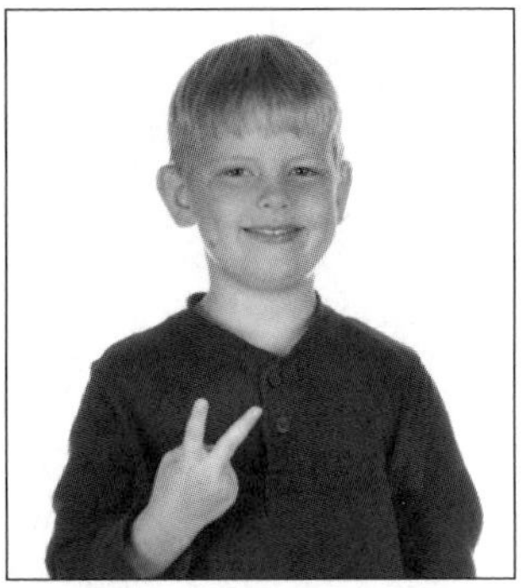

TWO: Hold up index and middle fingers with palm facing you.

Why It Works

Few kids can resist the rhythmic mayhem of the five little monkeys! You can make this a whole-body activity by inviting your child to jump while signing JUMP. Because it's so easy to produce the signs to follow the rhythm in this rhyme, using their whole bodies helps children internalize the rhythm of the spoken language! In addition, the strong rhythms emphasize the syllables of the words (for example, "Ma-ma called the doc-tor . . ."), helping children understand phonology.

A NOTE ABOUT THE SIGNS

Make sure you shake your head when signing the last line and use a stern expression to show the monkeys that you mean it! To make this rhyme even simpler for very young children, replace the signs in the last line with the finger shaking gesture.

READ AND SIGN TOGETHER!

For Babies and Toddlers

Five Little Monkeys Jumping on the Bed by Eileen Christelow. New York: Clarion, 1989.

Llama Llama Home with Mama by Anna Dewdney. New York: Viking, 2011.

Boo Hoo Bird by Jeremy Tankard. New York: Scholastic, 2009.

For Preschoolers

Farm Flu by Teresa Bateman. Morton Grove, IL: Albert Whitman, 2001.

Please Play Safe: Penguin's Guide to Playground Safety by Margery Cuyler. New York: Scholastic, 2006.

Officer Buckle and Gloria by Peggy Rathmann. New York: G. P. Putnam's Sons, 1995.

Feelings

If You're Happy and You Know It (ages two to six years)

(adapted traditional)

If you're HAPPY and you know it, clap your hands.
If you're HAPPY and you know it, clap your hands.
If you're HAPPY and you know it, then your SIGNS will surely show it.
If you're HAPPY and you know it, clap your hands.
If you're SAD and you know it, cry some tears . . .
If you're ANGRY and you know it, stomp your feet . . .
If you're SCARED and you know it, curl up into a ball . . .
If you're EXCITED and you know it, jump up and down . . .

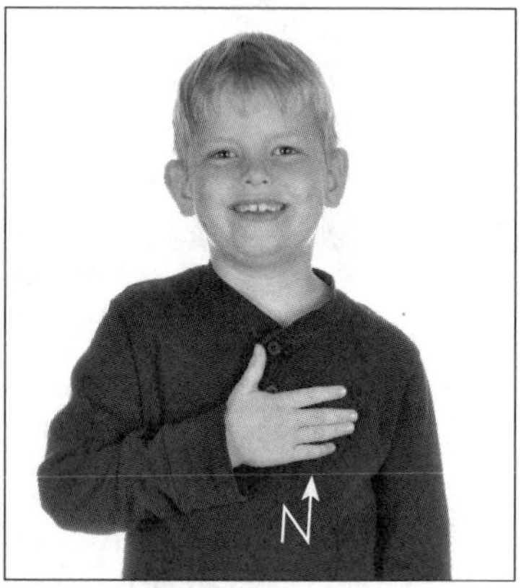

HAPPY: Brush a flat hand in an upward motion on your chest. Make sure your facial expression looks happy!

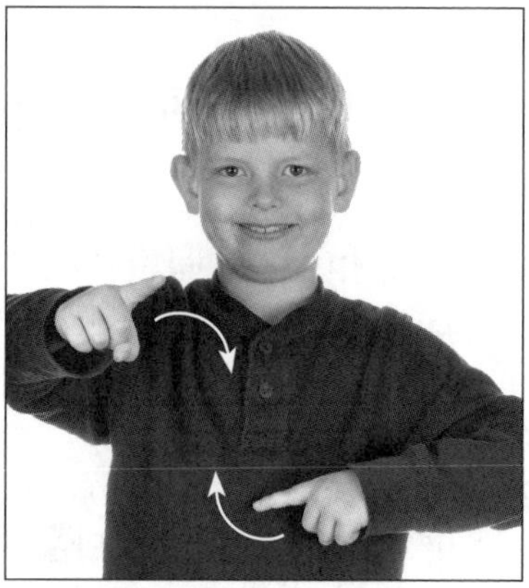

SIGN: Move index fingers in a circle back toward you.

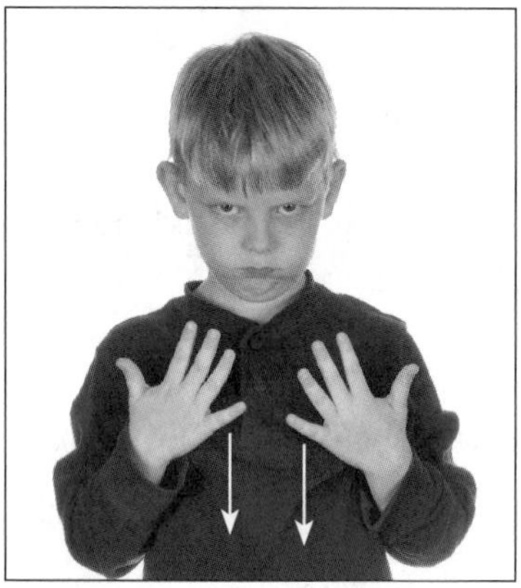

SAD: Hold both hands with palms facing you and fingers up. Move hands downward in front of face, with a sad facial expression.

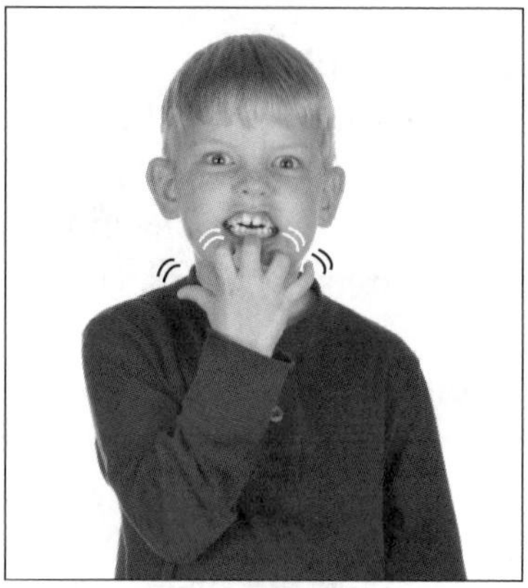

ANGRY: With an angry expression, make a claw handshape in front of your face and wiggle your fingers.

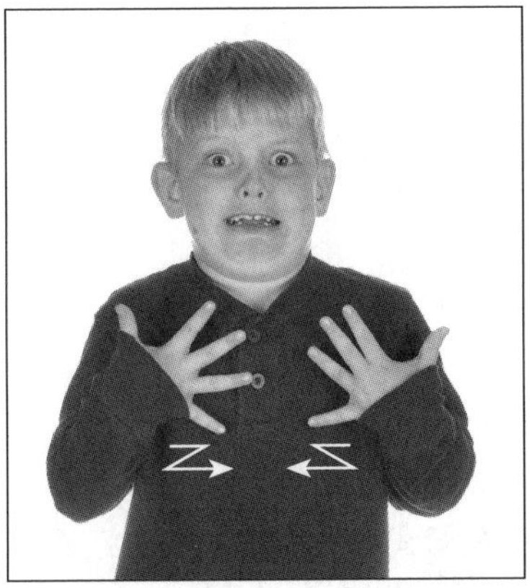

SCARED: Hold both hands sideways, with palms facing you. Move hands toward each other twice, with a frightened expression on your face.

EXCITED: With all your fingers up, bend the middle finger of each hand slightly forward. Brush hands alternately upward over chest, with an excited facial expression.

Why It Works

This active version of a storytime favorite engages kids through large motor movement while emphasizing the vocabulary of emotions. Young children often find themselves overwhelmed by feelings they cannot name. Because ASL signs for feelings tend to incorporate visual features of the feelings (such as the downward movement of SAD), they serve as visual cues for the feelings and allow kids to internalize the features of the feelings as they sign them. You can extend this activity by asking your child to describe other feelings and actions to go with them. Build text-to-self connections by describing specific times when you or your child experienced each feeling and how each of you behaved.

READ AND SIGN TOGETHER!

For Babies and Toddlers

The Runaway Bunny by Margaret Wise Brown. New York: HarperFestival, 2008.
Grumpy Bird by Jeremy Tankard. New York: Scholastic, 2007.
My Friend Is Sad by Mo Willems. New York: Hyperion, 2007.

For Preschoolers

Today I Feel Silly by Jamie Lee Curtis. New York: Joanna Cotler, 1998.
How Are You Peeling? by Saxton Freymann. New York: Scholastic, 1999.
When You Are Happy by Eileen Spinelli. New York: Simon and Schuster, 2006.

Manners

Taking Turns Bounce (ages birth to two years)

Put your child in your lap and bounce side to side to the rhythm as you say the rhyme.

TAKING-TURNS is fun to do.
First it's me (MY-TURN) and then it's you (YOUR-TURN).
Back and forth and to and fro,
MY TURN, YOUR TURN, here we go!
Now let's do it slowly! (*repeat the rhyme slowly*)
Now let's do it quickly! (*repeat the rhyme quickly*)

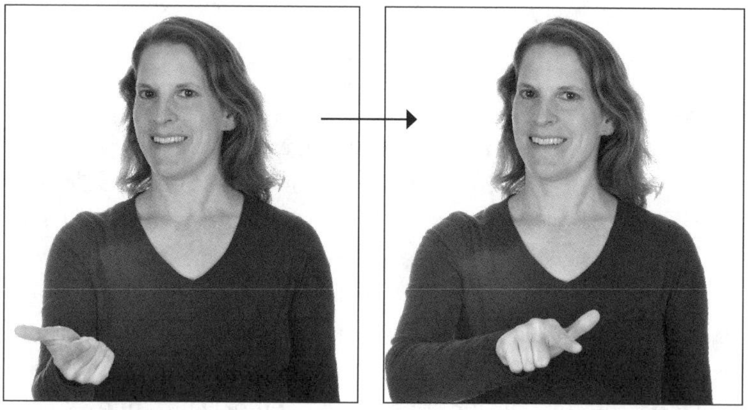

TAKE-TURNS: Move a sideways L-handshape back and forth between or among the people taking turns.

MY-TURN: Tip a sideways L-handshape toward your chest.

YOUR-TURN: Tip a sideways L-handshape toward the other person.

Why It Works

This activity allows your child to experience and internalize language with multiple senses—hearing the words in a rhythmic way, feeling the rhythm as you bounce her along, and seeing the signs. The back-and-forth nature of the rhyme and the bounce also emphasizes the directionality of the sign, so when you use it in context, your child will understand it clearly.

> **A NOTE ABOUT THE SIGNS**
>
> The sign TAKE-TURNS is a wonderful example of the economy of space and directionality in American Sign Language! When signing MY-TURN, the palm of the hand should be facing you. When signing YOUR-TURN, the back of your hand should be facing the person whose turn it is. You can also show a group of people taking turns by tipping the sign toward each person in turn.

Manners Song (ages one to six years)

(to the tune of "If You're Happy and You Know It")

To ask for something nicely I say PLEASE.
To ask for something nicely I say PLEASE.
I want to show good manners, yes I really want to show them,
So to ask for something nicely I say PLEASE.
When someone gives me something, I say THANK-YOU . . .
When I bump into someone, I say EXCUSE-ME . . .
When we're playing with our toys, we like to SHARE . . .
When I make a mistake, I say SORRY . . .

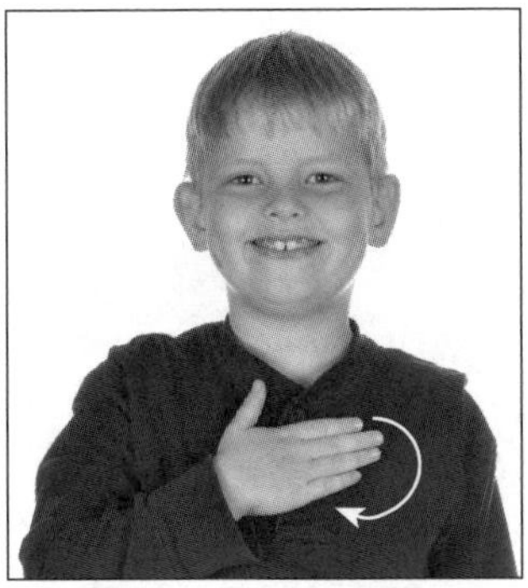

PLEASE: Move a flat hand in a circle over your chest.

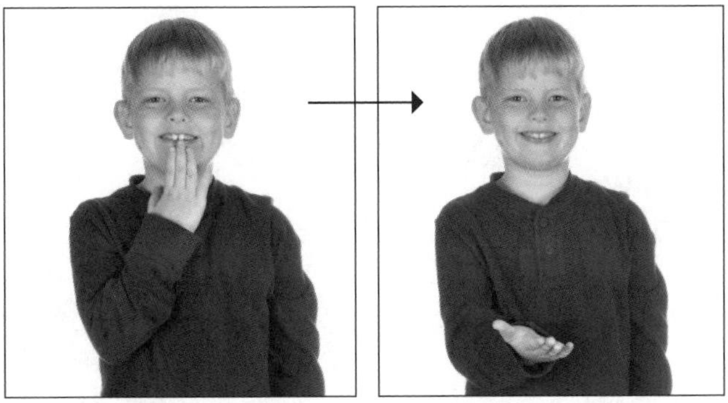

THANK-YOU: Touch the fingertips of a flat hand to your chin and then move them in the direction of the person you are addressing.

EXCUSE-ME: Hold one hand out flat with palm facing up. Bend fingers of the other hand and brush them several times across the palm of the first hand (as if brushing away the offensive thing you did).

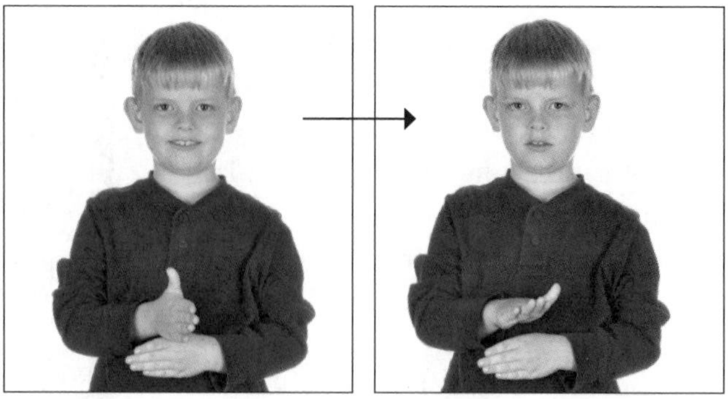

SHARE: Hold one flat hand sideways with the palm facing you. Hold the other flat hand above it, perpendicular to the first. Move the bottom edge of the upper hand from side to side, as if sweeping half of the thing you are sharing to one side and half to the other.

A NOTE ABOUT THE SIGNS

The fist handshape in the sign SORRY represents the letter *s* in American Sign Language, so this sign can help your child remember that the English word *sorry* begins with *s*.

SORRY: Make a fist and move it in a circle over your heart. Make sure your facial expression shows that you are sorry!

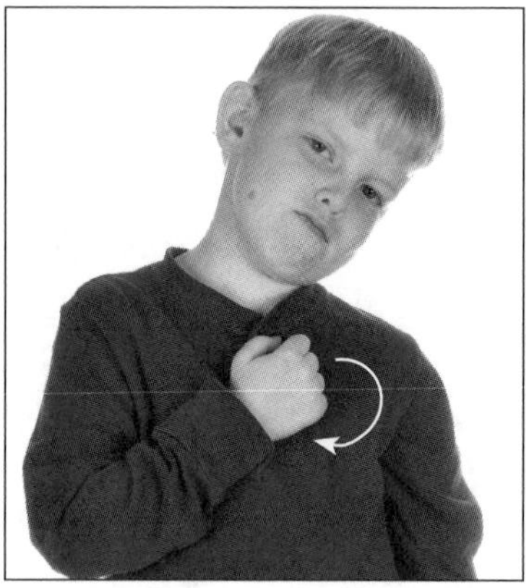

Why It Works

One of the most amazing things about signing with babies is seeing a very young child sign PLEASE or THANK-YOU. Be warned, though—it's so cute that many adults find it hard to say no! This activity is a fun and engaging way to introduce or reinforce manners signs, but, as young children learn best in context, make sure you also emphasize each sign in everyday situations. For example, each time you say "thank you" to your child, accompany it with the sign. To prompt your child to use the signs, slowly start to sign them yourself, with an expectant facial expression—he will quickly pick it up!

READ AND SIGN TOGETHER!

For Babies and Toddlers

Excuse Me: A Little Book of Manners by Karen Katz. New York: Grosset and Dunlap, 2002.

Say Please!: A Book about Manners by Tony Ross. La Jolla, CA: Kane/Miller, 2006.

How Do Dinosaurs Eat Their Food? by Jane Yolen. New York: Blue Sky, 2005.

For Preschoolers

Please Is a Good Word to Say by Barbara Joosse. New York: Philomel, 2007.

Suppose You Meet a Dinosaur: A First Book of Manners by Judy Sierra. New York: Knopf, 2012.

The Duckling Gets a Cookie!? by Mo Willems. New York: Hyperion, 2012.

Playtime

Roll the Ball (ages birth to three years)

(to the tune of "Row, Row, Row Your Boat")

Roll, roll, roll the BALL, HAPPY as can be,
(*Name*) rolls it back to me, quick as ONE TWO THREE.

BALL: Hold two claw-handshapes together as if holding a ball.

HAPPY: Brush a flat hand in an upward motion on your chest. Make sure your facial expression looks happy!

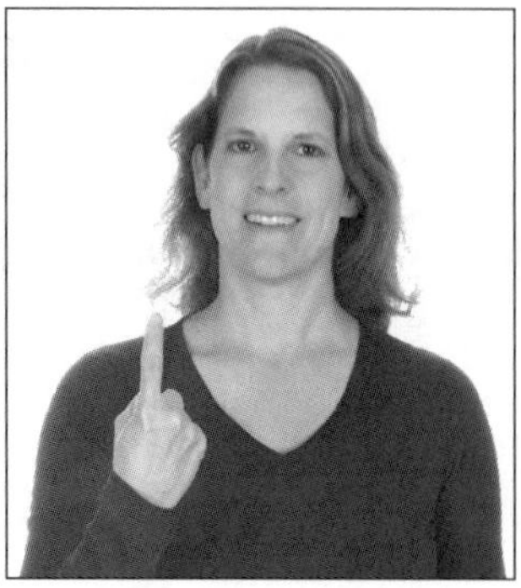

ONE: Hold up index finger with palm facing you.

TWO: Hold up index and middle fingers with palm facing you.

THREE: Hold up index and middle fingers and thumb with palm facing you.

Why It Works

Babies love balls! They also love interaction with caring adults, and that is what this song is really about. This back-and-forth game mimics the rhythm of communication.

Over the Candlestick (all ages)

Set an unlit candle on the floor and encourage your child to jump over the candle as you say the rhyme. If your child is too young to jump it, lift her over the candle. (Even the youngest babies enjoy this activity!)

Jack be NIMBLE, Jack be QUICK,
Jack jump over the candlestick [CANDLE JUMP-OVER].
Repeat with your child's name:
(*Name*) be NIMBLE, (*name*) be QUICK,
(*Name*) jump over the candlestick [CANDLE JUMP-OVER].

NIMBLE/GOOD AT: Make an F-handshape by bringing together your thumb and index finger. Holding your hand sideways, bring the tips of your index finger and thumb to your chin.

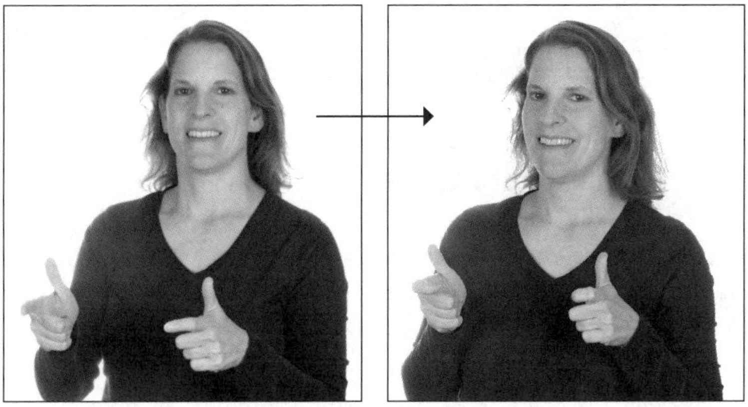

QUICK/FAST: Hold two sideways L-handshapes pointing out in front of you. Move them back toward you, curling your index fingers as you do so.

CANDLE: Hold up one index finger to represent the candle. Wiggle the fingers of your other hand on top of it to represent the flames.

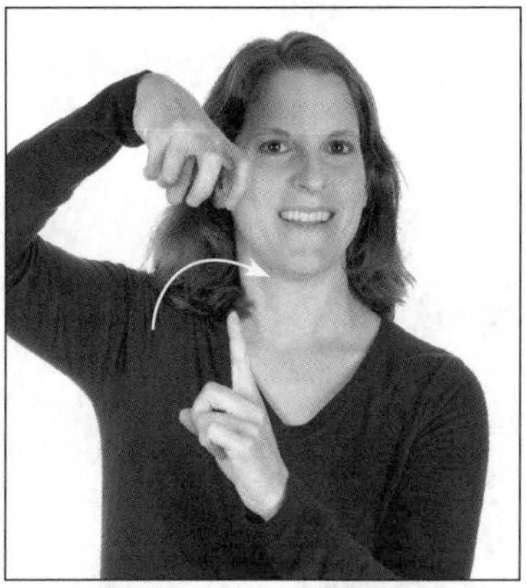

JUMP-OVER: Hold up one index finger to represent the candle. Make an upside-down V-handshape with the index finger and thumb of the other hand and then make it jump over the candlestick

Why It Works

Nursery rhymes are an important tool for spoken-language development because they incorporate rhythm, rhyme, and advanced vocabulary in context. By turning this nursery rhyme into an action rhyme, you allow your child to actively understand what the rhyme means. Using your child's name in the rhyme helps develop

A NOTE ABOUT THE SIGNS

In American Sign Language grammar, you must identify and establish an object before you can describe how someone interacted with it. (Because ASL is a visual language, this makes sense!) That's why we sign CANDLE first in this rhyme and then show the person jumping over it. Notice how the jumping is signed differently here than it is in "Five Little Monkeys" (p. 62)—this is another example of how ASL uses space so beautifully.

text-to-self connection, an important early literacy skill for understanding how words apply to everyday life.

The Where Game (ages one to three years)

This is a fun game that you can play almost anywhere, with almost anything! It's a great way to keep your child entertained while waiting in a doctor's office or a restaurant. Take a small object, such as a toy car, a doll, or even a shoe, and show it to your child. Then hide the object in a not-too-hard-to-find place. (Make sure children under twelve months actually see where you hide the object.) Sign "(object) WHERE." Let your child find the object (with help if necessary). Discuss where the object was found, including vocabulary relating it to other objects: "You're right! The CAR was under the chair!" Then sign YOUR-TURN, and let him have a turn hiding it. (Don't be surprised if very young children hide the object in exactly the same place you did!)

CAR: Hold fists in front of you and move them up and down as if holding a steering wheel.

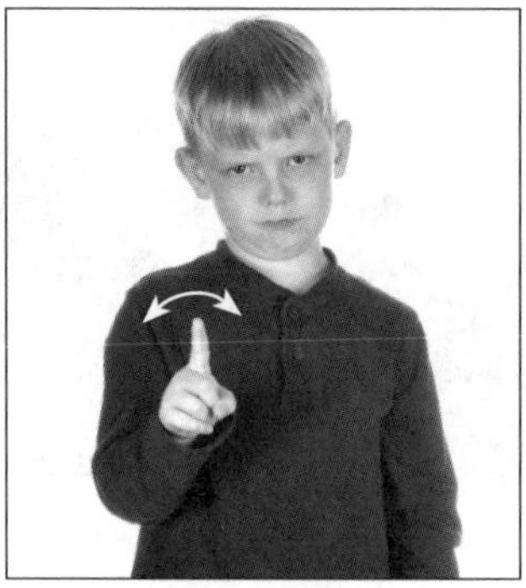

WHERE: With your palm facing out and your eyebrows furrowed, move your index finger from side to side.

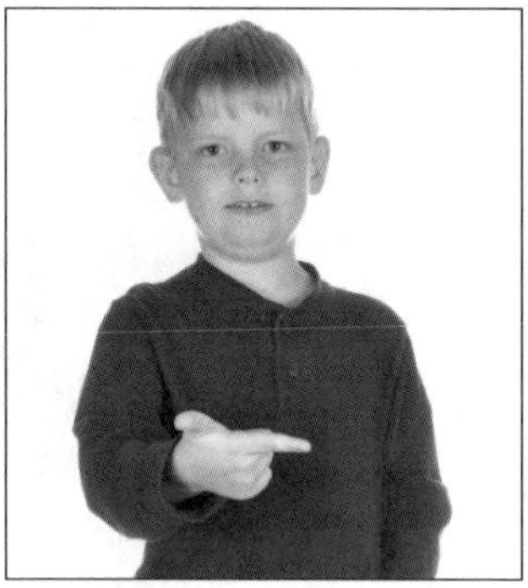

YOUR-TURN: Tip a sideways L-handshape toward the other person.

A NOTE ABOUT THE SIGNS

American Sign Language, like many languages around the world, is a topic-first language. That is why the sentence "Where is the car?" would be signed CAR WHERE? in ASL. Your child will benefit from signing with ASL structure, but will still benefit if you use your voice and sign, "WHERE is the CAR?" The most important thing is to show the question on your face: in this case, you would furrow your eyebrows for a "wh-word" question (who, what, where, when, why).

Why It Works

Infants under eight to twelve months old generally do not have an understanding of object permanence—that is, the idea that an object still exists even when you can't see it. That's why it's important to make sure that very young children actually see *where* you hide the object. As you play the game, you are reinforcing the idea in their minds that the object still exists when it is hidden, thus helping them develop object permanence. Narrating the finding of the object helps your child develop vocabulary, specifically in the realm of prepositions such as *over*, *under*, *next to*, and *behind*. Allowing your child to hide the object helps develop self-esteem and confidence.

Friends Sign Song (ages one to six years)

(to the tune of "Row, Row, Row Your Boat")

Here's the sign for YOU,
Here's the sign for ME,
I put my fingers together like this
'Cause FRIENDS we'll always be!

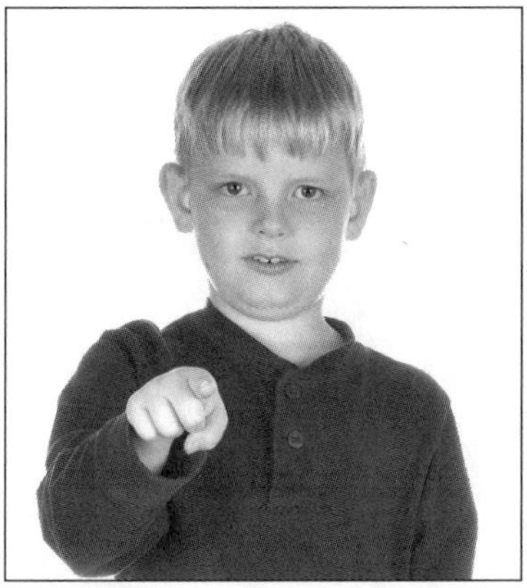

YOU: Point to the other person.

ME: Point to yourself.

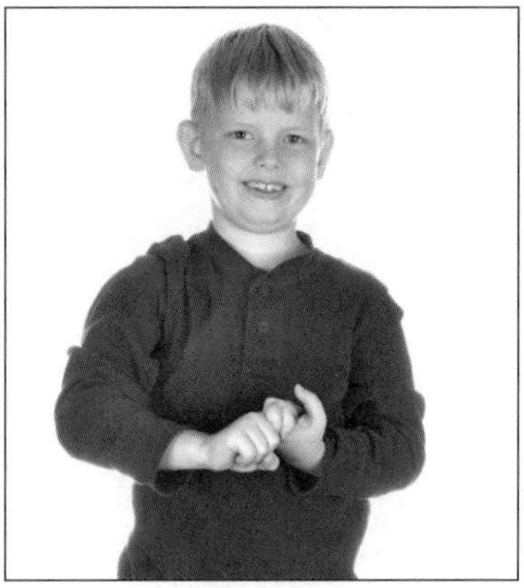

FRIEND: Link your index fingers and then turn your hands over and link your index fingers again.

A NOTE ABOUT THE SIGNS

Normally, when you sign a one-handed sign, you would use your dominant hand (or, in kids' terms, the hand you write with). In this song, I encourage kids to sign YOU with one hand and ME with the other, to emphasize how the two signs come together in a "hug" to form the sign FRIENDS.

Why It Works

"Piggyback songs," or songs that apply new lyrics to a well-known melody, are a wonderful way to help hearing children understand and remember new information. Kids tune in to sung information in a deeper way than they do with spoken information. So if you are tired of asking your child to pick up her toys, try making up a song about it! Singing about it, though often the last thing you feel like doing, pushes you and your child into a more playful place and helps reduce stress.

Similarly, sharing a story or visual hint about signs often helps children (and adults) remember what they mean. Though many ASL signs are iconic, meaning they look like what they mean, many more are not. So finding a related image, such as picturing two friends hugging for FRIENDS, will help you and your child remember the sign.

READ AND SIGN TOGETHER!

For Babies and Toddlers

Maisy Plays by Lucy Cousins. Cambridge, MA: Candlewick, 2001.
Kipper's Lost Ball by Mick Inkpen. New York: HMH Books, 2002.
I Can Share by Karen Katz. New York: Grosset and Dunlap, 2011.

For Preschoolers

What Shall We Play? by Sue Heap. Cambridge, MA: Candlewick, 2002.
Pete's a Pizza by William Steig. New York: HarperCollins, 1998.
Will You Be My Friend? by Nancy Tafuri. New York: Scholastic, 2000.

chapter 7

Out and About

AS CHILDREN GROW, THEIR WORLD EXPANDS AS THEY learn about their place in the community. Visiting the doctor, shopping at the grocery store, going to school—all contribute to the young child's sensory experience of the world. Continuing to use sign language when you are out and about enhances children's vocabulary and helps them make connections to what they already know—both important prereading skills. And of course, signing is totally portable. You can sign anywhere—at the park, at a friend's house, at church, in the car. All you need is your hands!

On the Town

This Is the Way Lap Bounce (ages birth to two years)

Bounce your child in your lap as you say this rhyme.

This is the way the BABIES ride: slowly, slowly.
This is the way the FIREFIGHTERS ride: quickly! quickly!
This is the way the MAIL CARRIER rides: ride and stop, ride and stop.

BABY: Hold arms as if rocking a baby.

FIREFIGHTER: Hold a flat hand to your forehead with the palm facing out to represent the front of the firefighter's helmet.

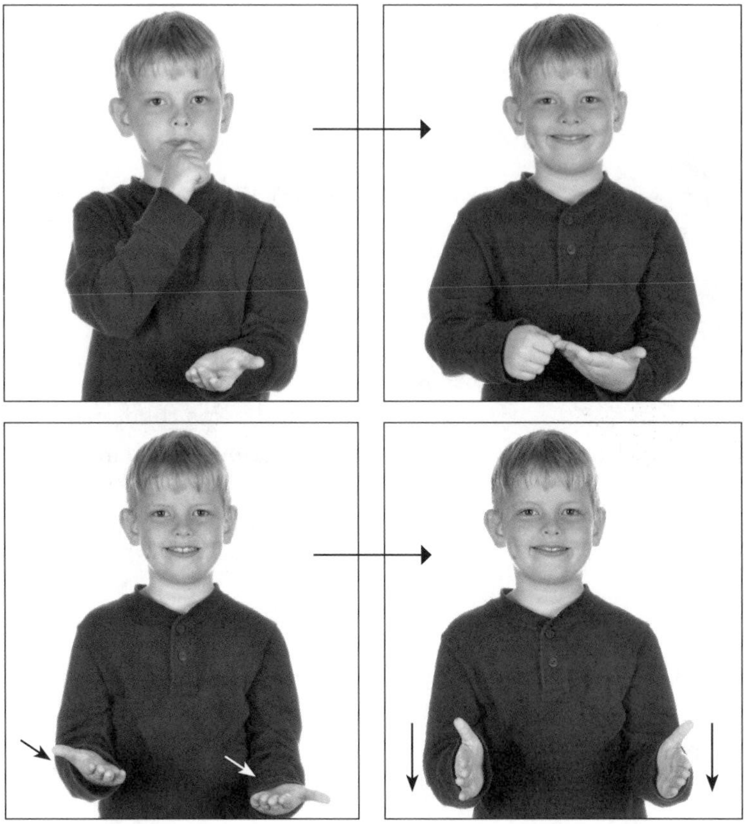

POSTMAN/LETTER CARRIER: Bend the fingers to the palm and bring the thumb to the mouth and then to the index finger of the other flat hand. This represents licking a stamp and putting it on an envelope and is the sign MAIL. Then hold both hands, palm up, to the side and bring them in front of you as if carrying something. Last, bring two flat hands, with palms facing each other, straight down to sign PERSON. These signs come together to make POSTMAN or LETTER CARRIER.

Why It Works

By combining rhythmic language with the large-scale movement of bouncing, this variation on the classic nursery rhyme "This Is the Way the Ladies Ride" engages babies to pay attention to the flow of language. The signs and concepts used here are ones from their everyday experience, and narrating the variations in movement enhances vocabulary.

Shhhhh! Everybody's Sleeping (ages two to six years)

In this delightful rhyming bedtime book by Julie Markes (New York: HarperCollins, 2004), community helpers snuggle up for bed in occupation-appropriate bedrooms. Use the signs for the different occupations as you read the book. After reading and signing the book a couple of times (because your child will ask for it again . . . and again), pause before saying or signing the name of the community helper to encourage your child to tell you what he sees.

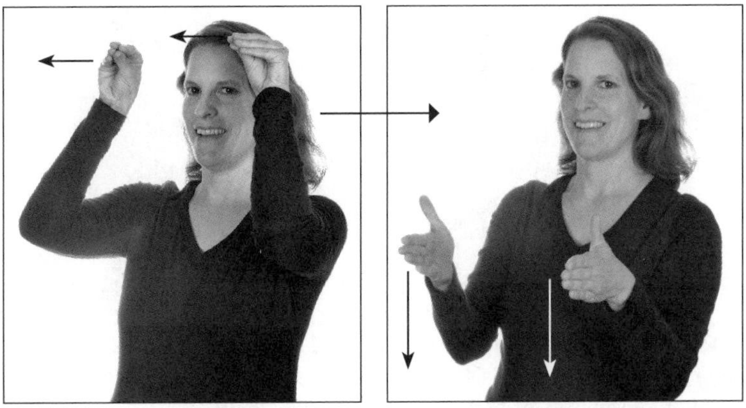

TEACHER: Bring fingers and thumb of each hand together and hold the backs of the hands near your forehead. Move your hands forward to sign TEACH. Then bring two flat hands, with palms facing each other, straight down to sign PERSON. These two signs together form TEACHER.

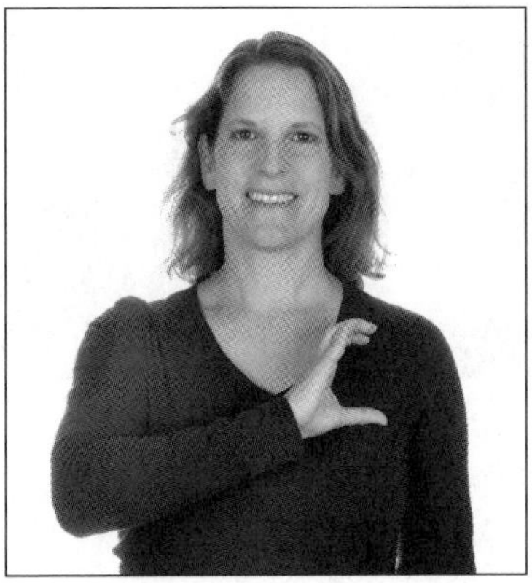

POLICE OFFICER: Make a C-handshape and hold it to your chest to represent the police officer's badge.

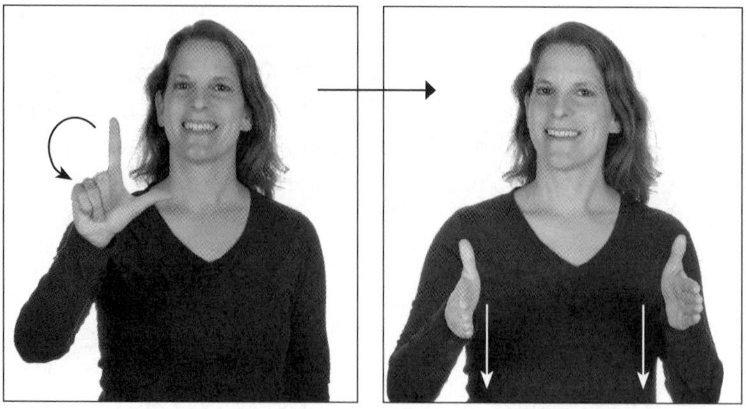

LIBRARIAN: Make an L-handshape and move it in a clockwise circle to sign LIBRARY. Then bring two flat hands, with palms facing each other, straight down to sign PERSON. These two signs together form LIBRARIAN.

FIREFIGHTER: Hold a flat hand to your forehead with the palm facing out to represent the front of the firefighter's helmet.

DOCTOR: Bring the bent fingers of one hand to the opposite wrist, as if checking a pulse.

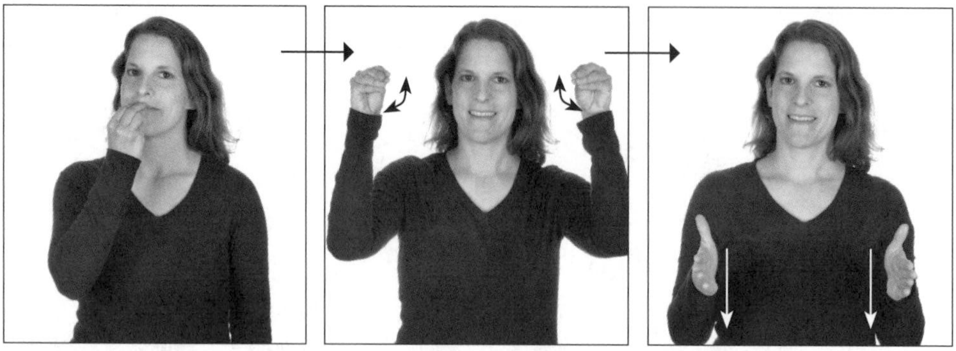

GROCER: Tap gathered fingertips and thumb to mouth to sign FOOD. Then bring gathered fingertips and thumbs of each hand up in front of you, with palms facing down, and move the hands forward and back to sign SELL. Last, bring two flat hands, with palms facing each other, straight down to sign PERSON. These three signs together form GROCER.

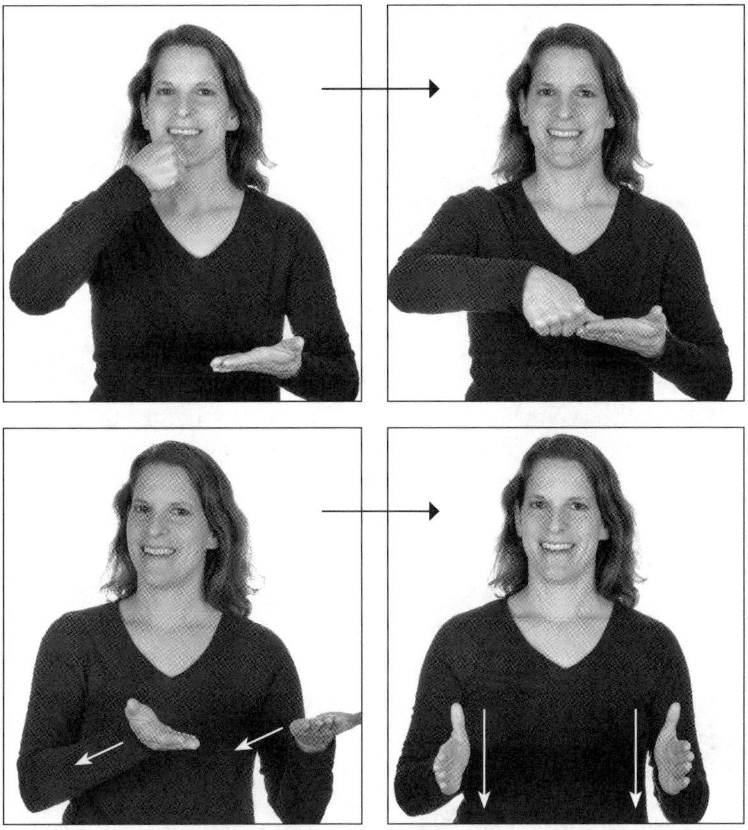

POSTMAN/LETTER CARRIER: Bend the fingers to the palm and bring the thumb to the mouth and then to the index finger of the other flat hand. This represents licking a stamp and putting it on an envelope and is the sign MAIL. Then hold both hands, palm up, to the side and bring them in front of you as if carrying something. Last, bring two flat hands, with palms facing each other, straight down to sign PERSON. These signs come together to make POSTMAN or LETTER CARRIER.

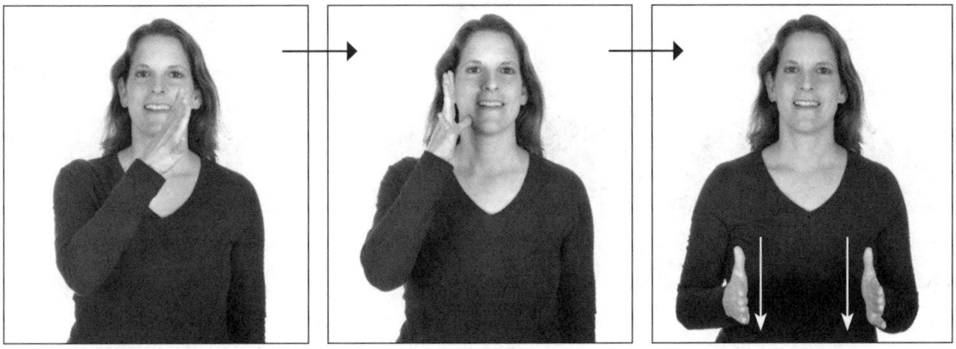

FARMER: Hold the thumb of a 5-handshape to the opposite side of the chin and then to the closer side, to sign FARM. Then bring two flat hands, with palms facing each other, straight down to sign PERSON. These two signs together form FARMER.

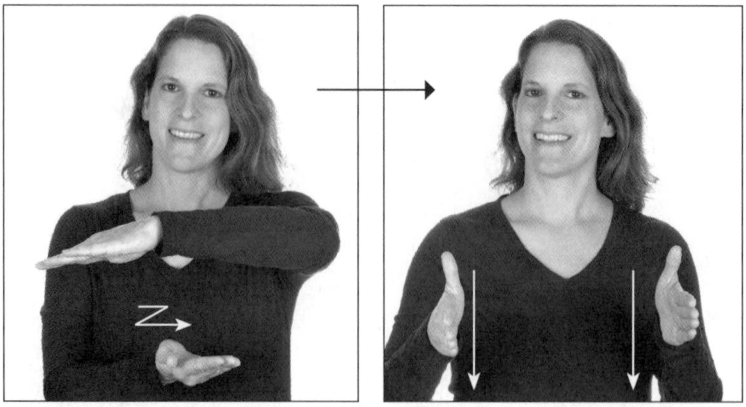

BAKER: Hold one arm horizontally in front of you to represent the oven and then use the flat hand of the other arm to put something in the oven. This is the sign BAKE. Then bring two flat hands, with palms facing each other, straight down to sign PERSON. These two signs together form BAKER.

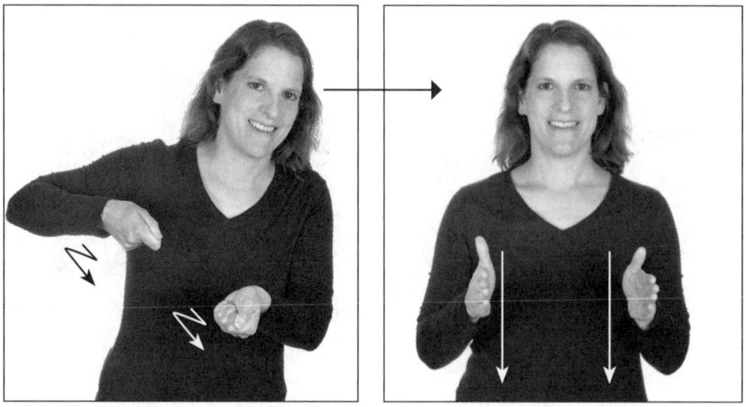

GARDENER: Mime using a hoe and then bring two flat hands, with palms facing each other, straight down to sign PERSON.

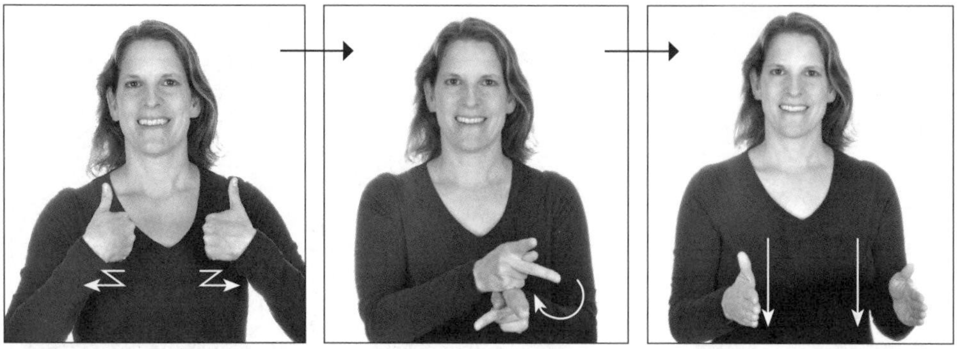

ZOOKEEPER: Bring the fingertips of both flat hands to your chest and move your wrists side to side to sign ANIMAL. Then hold up the index and middle fingers of each hand and bring your thumbs to rest between the fingers to make K-handshapes. Stack the K-handshapes and move them forward and back in a circular motion to form the sign TAKE-CARE-OF. Last, bring two flat hands, with palms facing each other, straight down to sign PERSON. These three signs together form the sign ZOOKEEPER.

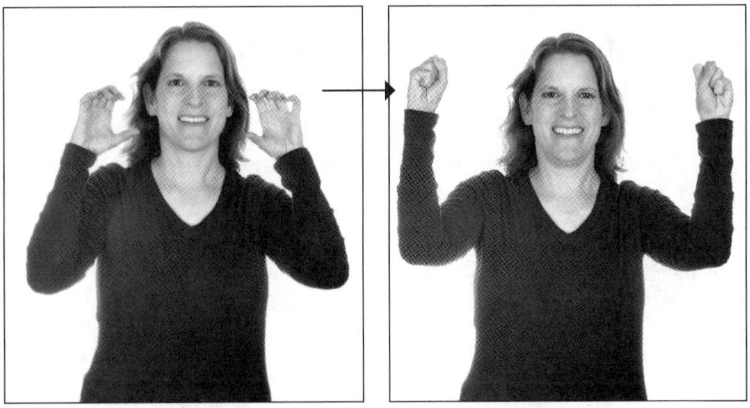

PRESIDENT: Hold two flat hands, palms facing forward, at your forehead. Move the hands up and away from you, closing them into fists as you do.

Why It Works

The bouncy, rhyming structure of this book is both soothing and engaging. The pictures are full of delightful visual details, from the librarian's bookshelf bed to the farmer's sheep pillow. Books that use a repetitive structure to introduce a series of thematically related items, like this one, are ideal for introducing and reinforcing ASL vocabulary. Reading the same story again and again helps children internalize concepts and language patterns, allowing them to develop competence and confidence.

A NOTE ABOUT THE SIGNS

Part of the sign ZOOKEEPER can mean to take care of someone or something. However, if you sign TAKE-CARE-OF briefly and adjust your facial expression, it means, "Be careful!"

What I'll Do Today Craft (ages three to six years)

This fun craft that you and your child can make together also serves a practical purpose: hang it on the fridge or in your child's bedroom to provide a visual cue about what to expect for the day.

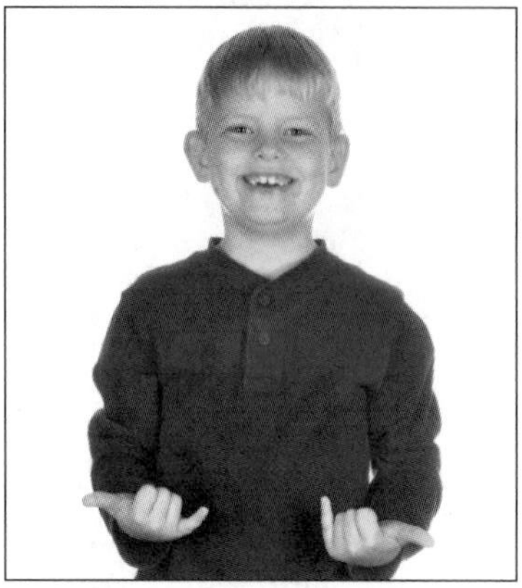

TODAY: Hold up thumb and pinky of each hand with palms facing you. Bring the hands in a slight downward motion at the waist.

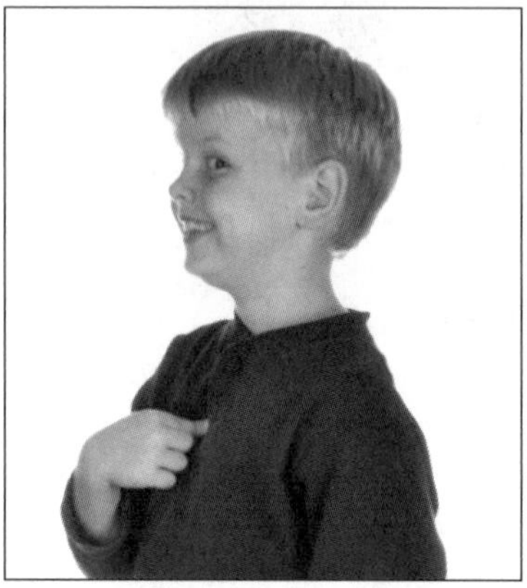

I: Point to yourself.

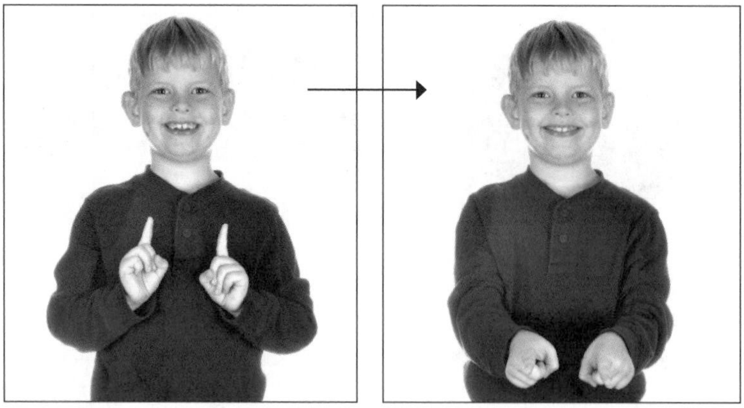

GO: Hold the index fingers of both hands up in front of you and then move them away and down in the direction you are going.

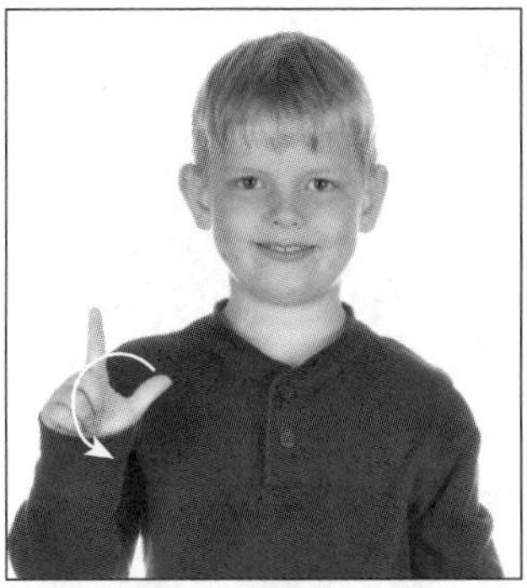

LIBRARY: Make an L-handshape and move it in a clockwise circle.

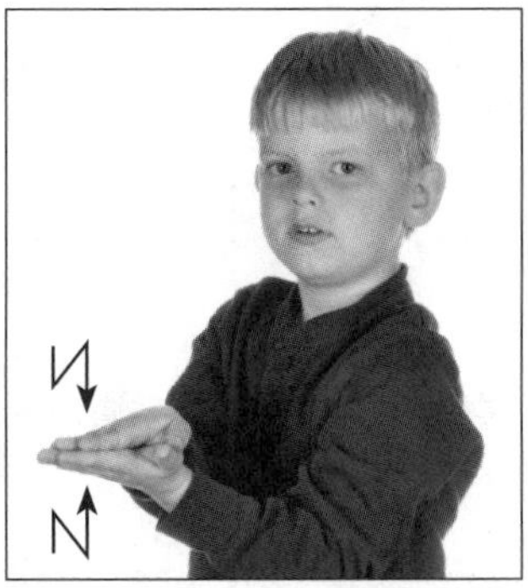

SCHOOL: Clap flat hands horizontally in front of you two times.

STORE: Bring gathered fingertips and thumbs of each hand up in front of you with palms facing down and then move the hands forward and back.

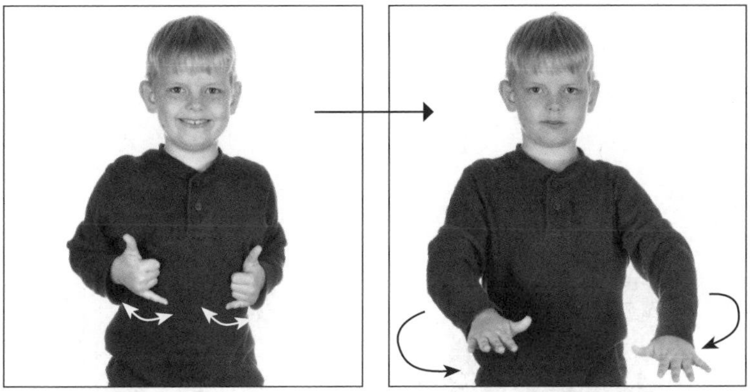

PLAYGROUND: Hold up the thumb and pinky of each hand and shake them back and forth to sign PLAY. Then move two flat hands, palms facing down, in a wide circular motion in front of you, to sign AREA. These two signs together form PLAYGROUND.

DOCTOR: Bring the bent fingers of one hand to the opposite wrist, as if checking a pulse.

DENTIST: Make a fist and then turn it so that your palm is facing you. Touch your pinky knuckle to the side of your mouth.

RESTAURANT: Twist your index and middle fingers together to make an R-handshape. Touch the R-handshape to the opposite side of your chin and then to the closer side.

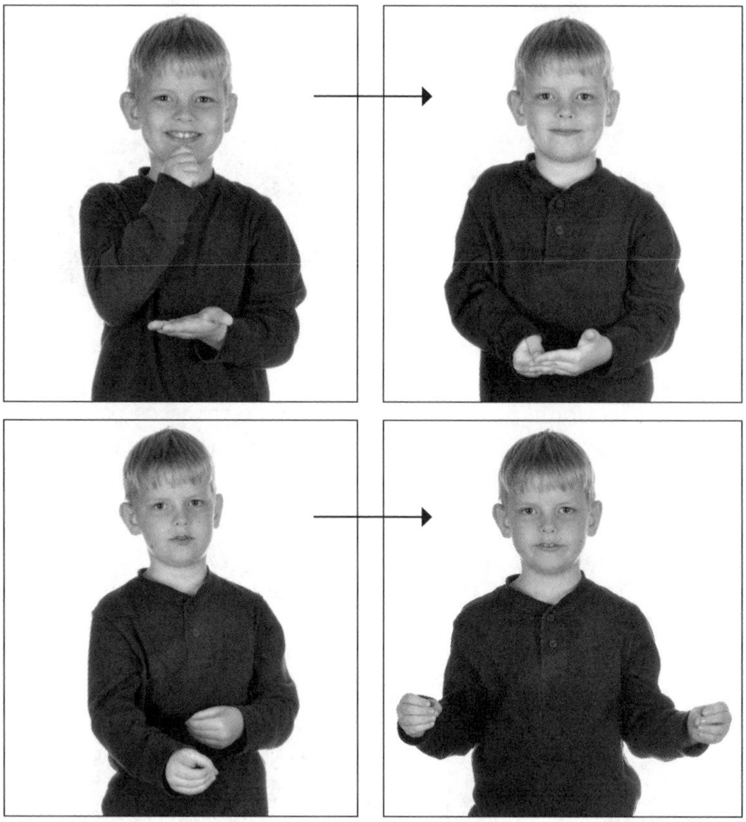

POST OFFICE: Bend the fingers to the palm and bring the thumb to the mouth and then to the index finger of the other flat hand. This represents licking a stamp and putting it on an envelope and is the sign MAIL. Next make two O-handshapes and hold them, both palms facing you, in front of your body, with one close to your stomach and one about six inches away. Then move the O-handshapes so that the palms face each other. This represents four walls and is the sign OFFICE. These signs come together to make POST OFFICE.

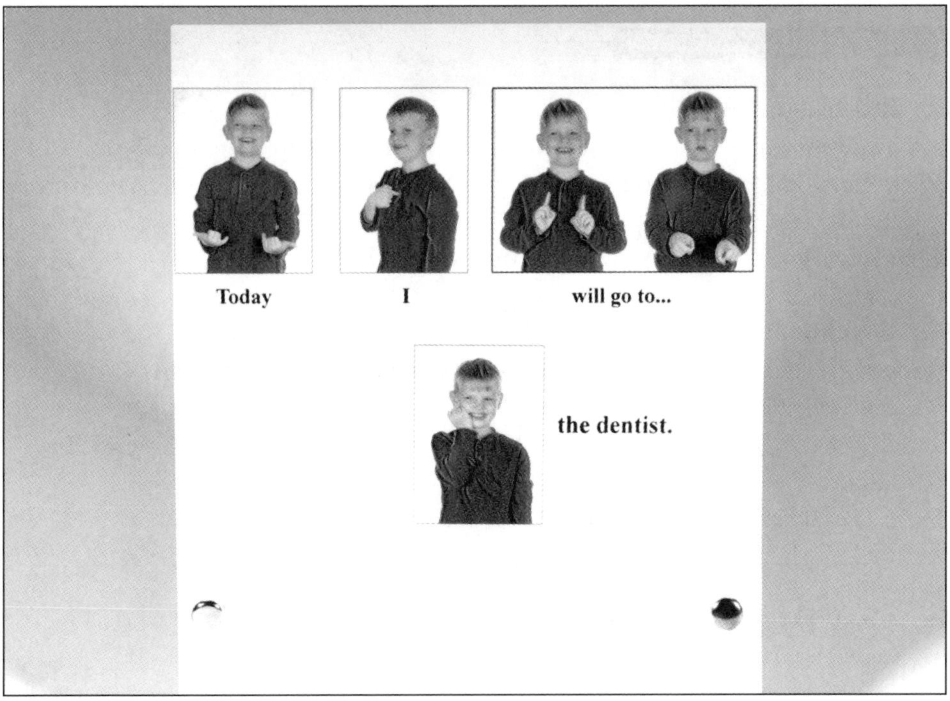
Today
I
will go to...
the dentist.

Directions:

1. Photocopy the template from appendix C. For a sturdier project, use cardstock instead of paper. Print the location cards sheet double-sided.
2. Cut out the chart page. Use a hole punch or a sharp pencil to poke holes where indicated. Fold up the bottom edge along the dotted line and then secure it with paper fasteners in the holes.
3. Decorate the chart with crayons or stickers, or both.
4. Cut out the location cards. Place them in the pocket of the chart so that today's destination shows above the pocket edge.

Why It Works

Discussing activities before they happen helps children feel secure and know what to expect. This chart is an excellent visual reminder, but you can use signs throughout the day to achieve the same effect. Teaching babies these signs allows them to be a part of the conversation—and they can even ask about the day's activities before they can speak. The more difficult the transition, the more important it is not to spring it on your child.

READ AND SIGN TOGETHER!

For Babies and Toddlers

My Neighborhood by Lisa Bullard. Minneapolis, MN: Picture Window, 2003.
Whose Hat Is This? by Sharon Katz Cooper. Minneapolis, MN: Picture Window, 2006.
Hi! by Ann Herbert Scott. New York: Puffin, 1997.

For Preschoolers

Be My Neighbor by Maya Ajmera and John D. Ivanko. Watertown, MA: Charlesbridge, 2005.
On the Town: A Community Adventure by Judith Caseley. New York: Greenwillow, 2002.
Career Day by Anne Rockwell. New York: HarperCollins, 2000.

In the Waiting Room

Waiting Song (ages one to six years)

(to the tune of "The Farmer in the Dell")

WAITING can be hard, so I SING a little song,
And now I'll SING in a SILLY way, and the WAIT won't seem so long!

Repeat the song singing like a duck, as if you are underwater, as if your teeth are glued together, and so on. Encourage your child to come up with ideas, and the wait will fly by!

WAIT: Hold both hands in front of you with palms facing you. Wiggle the fingers.

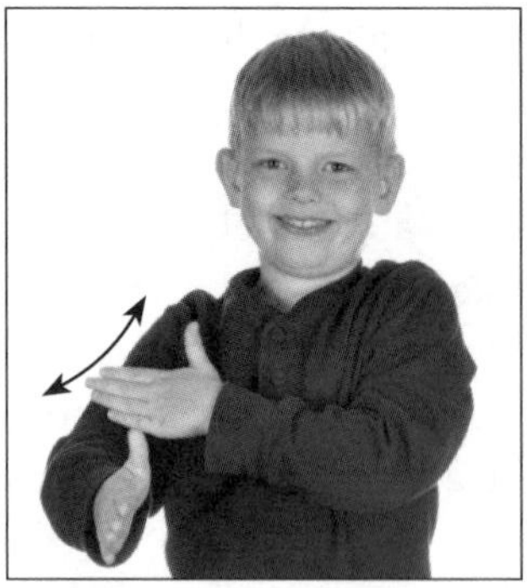

SING: Hold up one arm horizontally. Move the flat palm of the other hand back and forth in the air over the arm.

SILLY: Hold up your thumb and pinky in front of your face so that your thumb is near your nose. Wiggle your hand back and forth and make a silly face.

Why It Works

Because it's so silly, of course! What child can resist singing like a duck? Making your child an active participant in the song immediately engages him and helps develop creativity, not to mention the flexibility in thinking born of language play. This song works especially well for families with children of multiple ages: babies will avidly watch to see what crazy thing their families will do next, all the while basking in the language play and being soothed by the music, and older children will be engaged by the silliness and the opportunity to try out new ways of singing. (And if you are afraid of the silliness getting out of hand, just direct it to a quieter place: "Now let's sing and sign like a teeny little ant!")

ASL ANYWHERE

Got some time to kill in the waiting room or at a restaurant? Here are some other entries in this book you can use to engage your child with minimal materials:

Brush Your Teeth (p. 46)
The Where Game (p. 74)
Ride Your Bike (p. 90)
Caterpillar Tickle (p. 96)
The Alphabet Game (p. 109)
My Bouncing Buckaroo (p. 111)
I Spy (p. 114)

READ AND SIGN TOGETHER!

For Babies and Toddlers

Maisy, Charley, and the Wobbly Tooth by Lucy Cousins. Cambridge, MA: Candlewick, 2006.
Corduroy Goes to the Doctor by Don Freeman. New York: Viking, 1987.
Let's Get a Checkup by Alan Katz. New York: Little Simon, 2010.

For Preschoolers

Dinner at the Panda Palace by Stephanie Calmenson. New York: HarperCollins, 1991.
Next Please by Ernst Jandl. New York: G. P. Putnam's Sons, 2003.
Freddie Visits the Dentist by Nicola Smee. New York: Little Barron's, 2000.

Transportation

Ride Your Bike (ages two to six years)

(to the tune of "Row, Row, Row Your Boat")

Ride, ride, ride your BIKE, riding to and fro.
When the light is GREEN we know that now it's time to go.
Ride, ride, ride your BIKE, riding through the town.
When the light is YELLOW, we know it's time to slow down.
Ride, ride, ride your BIKE, riding to the shop.
When the light is RED we know that now it's time to stop.

BICYCLE: Hold two fists in front of you and pedal them forward in a circular motion.

GREEN: Hold up index finger and thumb to make a G-handshape and then shake it.

YELLOW: Hold up pinky and thumb to make a Y-handshape and then shake it.

RED: Rub index finger downward over bottom lip.

Why It Works

You can use this activity with young children of any age. When singing this song with an infant, place your child on her back and bicycle her legs as you sing. (This is a great way to relieve gassy tummies!) Encourage toddlers and preschoolers to sign BIKE with you as you sing the song, varying the speed of the sign as the light turns from green to yellow to red. Follow up with a game that encourages concentration and visual acuity: you play the part of the light, while your child signs BIKE. She must watch you to see if she should sign it quickly (when you sign GREEN), slowly (when you sign YELLOW), or if she should stop (when you sign RED). Then let your child take a turn being the stoplight—this opportunity will develop confidence and help your child practice colors and color signs.

Vehicle Peek-a-Boo (ages one to three years)

Use pictures of vehicles, toy vehicles, or actual vehicles to introduce transportation signs to your child in everyday contexts such as while running errands or reading stories. Then play this fun guessing game anytime! To play, set out toy vehicles or pictures of vehicles. Hold each one up and show the sign for it. Then ask your child to cover his eyes (or gently cover them for him) and place one vehicle behind your back. Have him open his eyes and then ask, "Which one went away?" Encourage your child to answer with words or signs or both. When he does, pull out the vehicle and model a sentence: "Yes, the TRUCK drove away!" The beauty of this game is that it can grow with your child. For babies and toddlers, limit the choices to two or three vehicles each time you play the game. For older children, gradually increase the number of vehicles to increase the challenge.

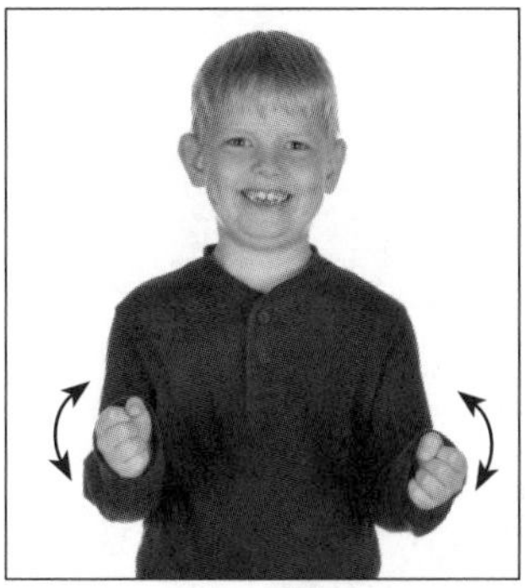

CAR: Hold fists in front of you and move them up and down as if holding a steering wheel.

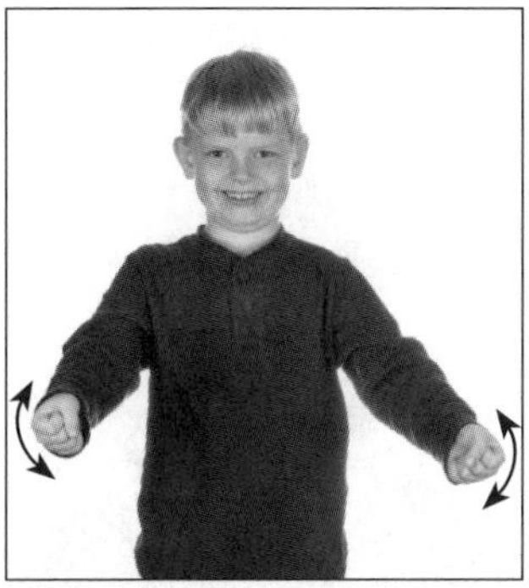

TRUCK: Hold fists down in front of you and move them as if holding a very large steering wheel.

TRAIN: Hold up the index and middle fingers of each hand to make U-handshapes. Turn both hands so that palms face down and move one U-handshape back and forth along the back of the other U-handshape.

AIRPLANE: Hold up your thumb, pinky, and index finger and turn your hand so your palm faces downward. Move your hand forward and back twice.

HELICOPTER: Hold one 5-handshape in front of you with your palm facing you. Place the other 5-handshape on the top of the thumb and wiggle it to represent a propeller.

DIGGER: Hold one hand out flat in front of you with the palm facing up. Pull a claw-handshape back toward you over the flat palm.

Why It Works

This game enhances memory, noticing, and visual acuity. Repetition of the game increases confidence and encourages verbal and signed interaction, which enhances communication skills and turn-taking in conversation.

ASL Boat Craft (ages two to six years)

This craft, which demonstrates the ASL sign BOAT, is simple enough for toddlers to complete with help and engaging enough for kindergarteners.

BOAT: Cup your hands together to make the shape of a boat.

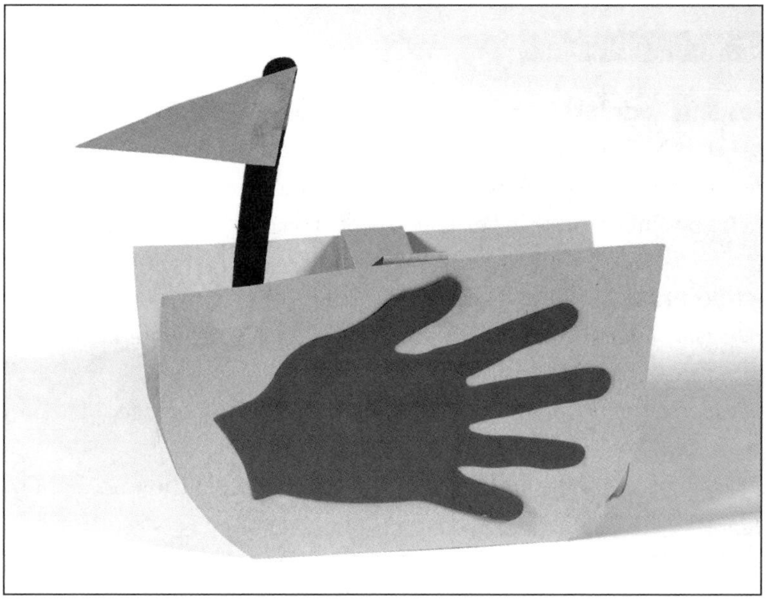

Directions:

1. Photocopy the template from appendix C. For a sturdier craft, print the template on cardstock or construction paper.
2. Cut out the boat shape, center piece, and flag along the black lines. (Precut these pieces for younger children.)
3. Fold the large boat piece in half along the dotted line.
4. Fold up the ends of the center piece along the dotted lines.
5. Glue the folded ends of the center piece to the inside edges of the boat so that the center piece holds the sides of the boat apart.
6. Use glue or tape to attach the flag piece to the end of a craft stick or straw and then attach the craft stick or straw to the inside of the boat.
7. Trace your child's hands onto construction paper and cut out the shapes.
8. Glue the hand shapes to the sides of the boat so that they show the sign BOAT. (Make sure both thumbs are facing up and the fingers are pointing in the same direction.)
9. Decorate as desired!

Why It Works

Crafts are a wonderful vehicle for language development—you can talk about the directions, narrate the sequence of events, and encourage your child to talk about the craft as he shows off the completed work. Don't forget—every boat needs a name! Encourage your child to give his boat a name and write it on the side in whatever way he likes.

READ AND SIGN TOGETHER!

For Babies and Toddlers

The Bridge Is Up! by Babs Bell. New York: HarperCollins, 2004.
Peek-a-Choo-Choo! by Maria Torres Cimarusti. New York: Dutton, 2007.
I Love Trucks! by Philemon Sturges. New York: HarperCollins, 1999.

For Preschoolers

How Will We Get to the Beach? A Guessing Game Story by Brigitte Luciani. New York: NorthSouth Books, 2000.
The Journey Home from Grandpa's by Jemima Lumley. Cambridge, MA: Barefoot Books, 2006.
Watch Me Go! Sign Language for Vehicles by Dawn Babb Prochovnic. Edina, MN: ABDO, 2010.

Nature

Day and Night Song (all ages)

(to the tune of "For He's a Jolly Good Fellow")

The SUN comes up in the MORNING, The SUN comes up in the MORNING,
The SUN comes up in the MORNING, That's how we know it's day.

The MOON comes out in the NIGHT time, The MOON comes out in the NIGHT time,
The MOON comes out in the NIGHT time, That's how we know it's night.

The STARS come out in the NIGHT time, The STARS come out in the NIGHT time,
The STARS come out in the NIGHT time,That's how we know it's night.

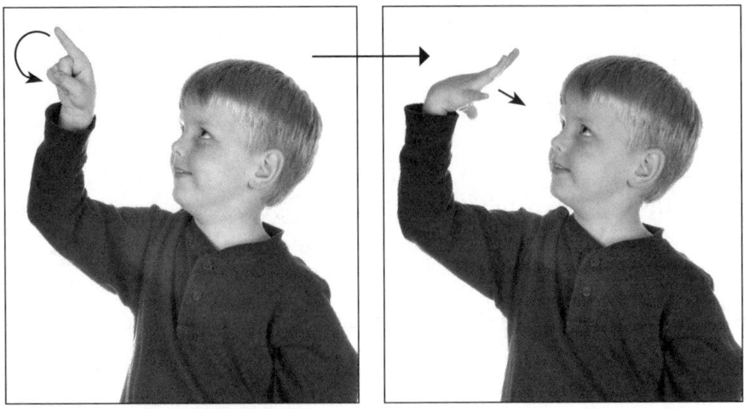

SUN: Draw a circle in the air with your index finger and then spread fingers toward your face to represent the rays of the sun.

MORNING: Hold one forearm parallel to the front of your body. Bring the inside elbow of the other arm to the fingertips of the first, with your flat hand held facing up. Move the hand upward to imitate the rising of the sun.

MOON: Make a crescent moon shape with your thumb and index finger. Hold it up to your eye and then up to the sky.

NIGHT: Hold one forearm parallel to the front of your body. Bend the fingers of the other hand forward and curve them over the first hand, to show the sun going down.

STAR: Hold index fingers together pointing up and then move them up and down in alternating motions. Look up at the stars as you make this sign

A NOTE ABOUT THE SIGNS

In American Sign Language, eye gaze is an important concept. A signer draws attention to important parts of the message by directing her eye gaze to it and uses eye gaze to share important information about spatial relationships. (This eye movement is part of the inherent grammar of American Sign Language.) When signing SUN, MOON, and STARS, make sure to look up!

Why It Works

This song introduces basic scientific concepts about day and night in an engaging way. The foundations of scientific curiosity are laid in infancy and toddlerhood when you encourage your child to make observations about the natural world.

Caterpillar Tickle (ages birth to two years)

Here comes the CATERPILLAR creeping along
Inch by inch as he sings this song:
La-di-da-di, La-di-da-di, La-di-da-di-dose,
Now giggle as the caterpillar tickles your nose!
(wiggle index finger over child's nose)

Repeat with other body parts, adjusting the nonsense words as needed.

CATERPILLAR: Hold one arm horizontally in front of you. Make the index finger of the other hand crawl up your arm to represent a caterpillar on a branch.

Why It Works

This simple tickle rhyme is perfect for babies of any age, and even toddlers and preschoolers love its silliness. The matching rhythms of the words and the movements of the caterpillar as he closes in for the tickle help babies internalize the rhythms of spoken language, and the suspense of finding out where the caterpillar will go next engages and entertains. This rhyme also emphasizes vocabulary for body parts, which is an important building block for language in the toddler years.

Animal Bounce (ages birth to two years)

Hold your baby in your lap and bounce to the rhythm as you chant and sign this animal rhyme!

This is the way the BUNNIES hop: hop hop hop hop! *(small bounces)*
This is the way the FROGGIES jump: jump jump jump jump! *(bigger bounces)*
This is the way the BIRDIES fly: up, up, up and away! *(lift your baby into the air)*

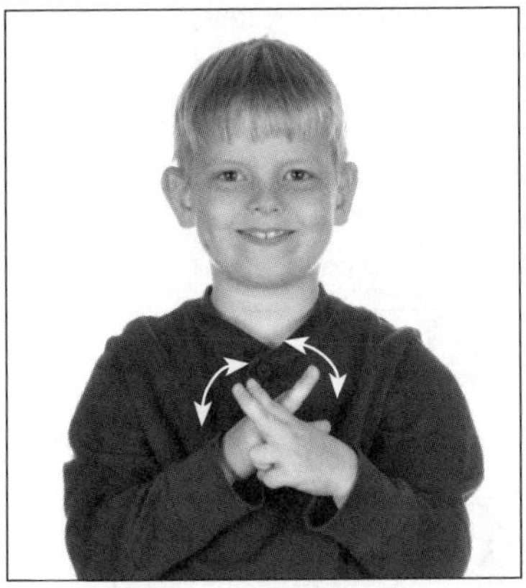

RABBIT: Hold up the index and middle fingers of each hand. Line up your hands next to each other so that the palms are facing away from each other and then flap your fingers to represent the rabbit's ears.

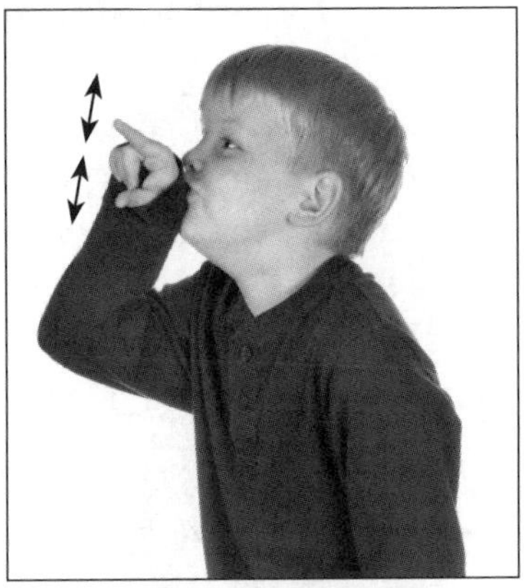

BIRD: With palm facing away from you and hand held in front of mouth, open and close your index finger and thumb to represent a beak.

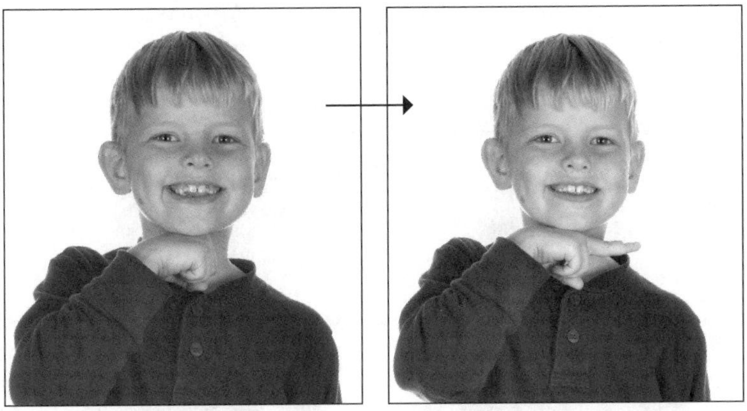

FROG: Make a fist and hold it under your chin. Then flick out your index and middle fingers.

Why It Works

Lap bounces are a time-honored way of engaging and calming a fussy baby and enhancing bonding. When you chant a rhythmic rhyme like this while bouncing your child, you are giving her a multisensory experience of language: seeing the signs, hearing the words, and feeling the rhythm of spoken language—not to mention the animal and movement vocabulary that she is taking in. What seems like a simple little rhyme to keep baby occupied is actually a catalyst for language development!

I Went Walking (ages one to four years)

In this book by Sue Williams (San Diego: Harcourt, 1989), a young child takes a walk on the farm and meets a menagerie of colorful animals. With its repetitive structure, this is a great book for sharing signs.

CAT: Pinch thumb and index finger together and brush them across your cheek to represent whiskers.

COW: Hold up thumb and pinky to make a Y-handshape. Hold the Y-handshape so that your thumb touches your temple.

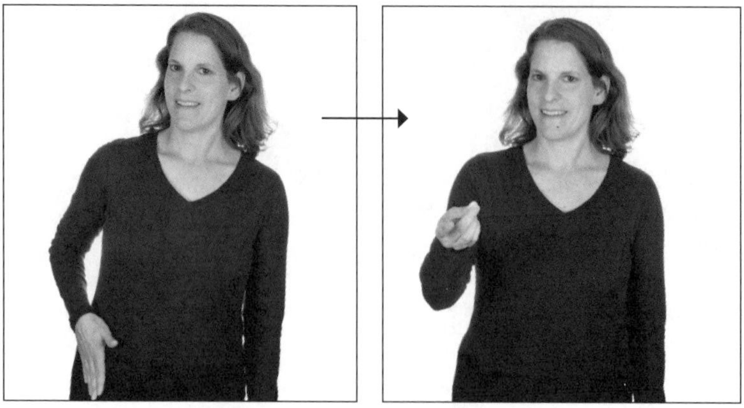

DOG: Tap your leg and snap your fingers as if calling a dog.

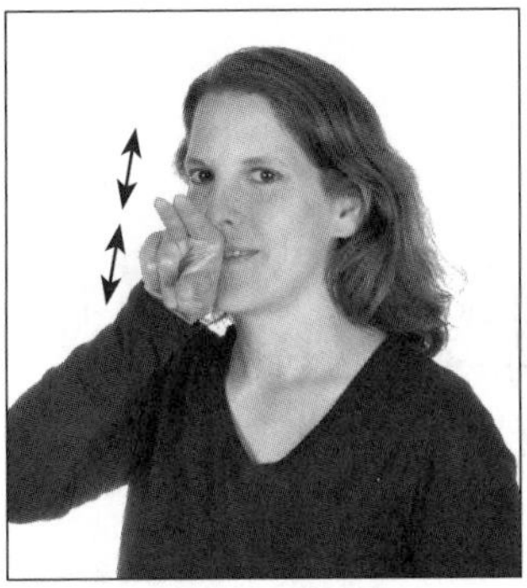

DUCK: With palm facing away from you and hand held in front of mouth, open and close your index and middle fingers and thumb to represent a duck's beak.

HORSE: Hold up your index and middle fingers and thumb. Place your thumb at your forehead and flap the fingers up and down to represent a horse's ear.

PIG: Hold a flat hand under your chin and bend your fingers up and down twice.

Why It Works

With large, bright illustrations on a simple white background, this book is wonderful for babies and toddlers. With the addition of signs to learn, older children will be equally engaged, making this a great choice to share with siblings of various ages. You can choose to use only color signs, only animal signs, or both. As you read, pause to ask your child to make predictions about what animals will come next. Interactions like these model the prediction and reading processes for young children.

READ AND SIGN TOGETHER!

For Babies and Toddlers

Peek-a-Moo by Maria Torres Cimarusti. New York: Dutton, 1998.

Early Sign Language: Signs for Pets and Animals. Eugene, OR: Garlic Press, 2002.

I Kissed the Baby! by Mary Murphy. Cambridge, MA: Candlewick, 2003.

For Preschoolers

1, 2, 3, to the Zoo! by Eric Carle. New York: Puffin, 1998.

Outside Your Window: A First Book of Nature by Nicola Davies. Somerville, MA: Candlewick, 2012.

The Seals on the Bus by Lenny Hort. New York: Henry Holt, 2000.

Seasons

Winter Snow (all ages)

It's WINTER time, and how the wind does blow.
It's WINTER time, and now here comes the SNOW!
It falls on the ground, it falls on my toes,
It falls on my tummy, it falls on my nose!

WINTER/COLD: Hold fists up in front of you and shiver.

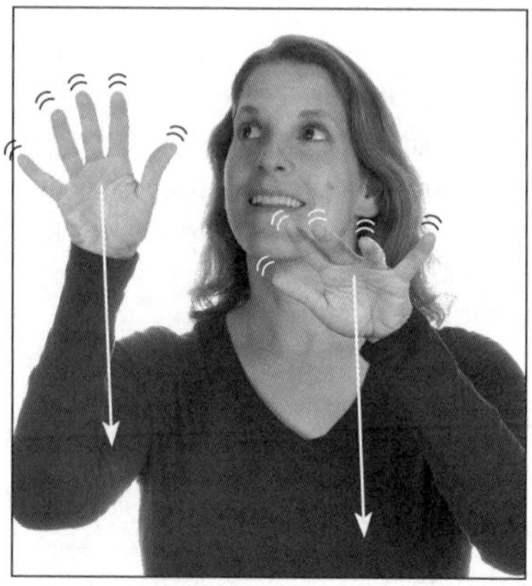

SNOW: Hold up hands with palms facing down and bring hands downward while you wiggle your fingers.

Why It Works

WINTER and SNOW are both great examples of iconic signs, or signs that look like what they mean. WINTER (this is also the sign for COLD) shows shivering, while SNOW shows flakes gently floating to the ground. This rhyme is a fun way to play with language, as you change the ending location of the sign SNOW to show where the snow is falling. Encourage your child's expressive language skills by asking for additional locations where the snow can fall. Sign them together, emphasizing words for body parts.

READ AND SIGN TOGETHER!

For Babies and Toddlers

Time to Sleep by Denise Fleming. New York: Henry Holt, 1997.
I See Winter by Charles Ghigna. Mankato, MN: Picture Window, 2012.
Kipper's Snowy Day by Mick Inkpen. San Diego, CA: Harcourt, 1996.

For Preschoolers

Bear in Long Underwear by Todd H. Doodler. Maplewood, NJ: Blue Apple, 2011.
Snowballs by Lois Ehlert. New York: Sandpiper, 1999.
The Snowy Day by Ezra Jack Keats. New York: Viking, 1962.

Autumn Leaves (all ages)

(to the tune of "London Bridge")

AUTUMN LEAVES are falling down,
Falling down, falling down. (Sign LEAF so that it falls to the floor.)
AUTUMN LEAVES are falling down,
RED, YELLOW, ORANGE, and BROWN.

AUTUMN: Brush the fingers of one hand along the back of the opposite forearm, as if brushing leaves away.

LEAF: Place a 5-handshape on the extended index finger of the other hand to represent a leaf on its stem.

RED: Rub index finger downward over bottom lip.

YELLOW: Hold up pinky and thumb to make a Y-handshape and then shake it.

ORANGE: Hold an O-handshape in front of your mouth and then squeeze as if squeezing an orange.

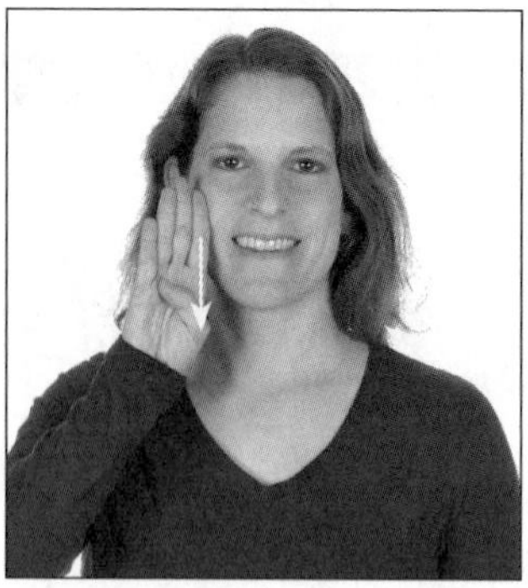

BROWN: Hold all four fingers together and fold thumb over palm to make a B-handshape. Move the B-handshape downward by your cheek.

Why It Works

Piggyback songs such as this one, which set new words to familiar tunes, are a great way to present new information or help remember something important. Need to engage your preschooler in the grocery store? Ask him to help you set your grocery list to a familiar song. Even better, sign it as you go. Bet you remember everything and get out of the store with fewer hassles!

READ AND SIGN TOGETHER!

For Babies and Toddlers

Fall Leaves Fall by Zoe Hall. New York: Scholastic, 2000.
Apples and Pumpkins by Anne Rockwell. New York: Macmillan, 1989.
Mouse's First Fall by Lauren Thompson. New York: Simon and Schuster, 2006.

For Preschoolers

Clifford's First Autumn by Norman Bridwell. New York: Scholastic, 1997.
When Autumn Falls by Kelly Nidey. Morton Grove, IL: Albert Whitman, 2004.
Leaves! Leaves! Leaves! by Nancy Elizabeth Wallace. New York: Marshall Cavendish, 2003.

Spring Flower Craft (ages three to six years)

This surprising craft shows the sign I-LOVE-YOU!

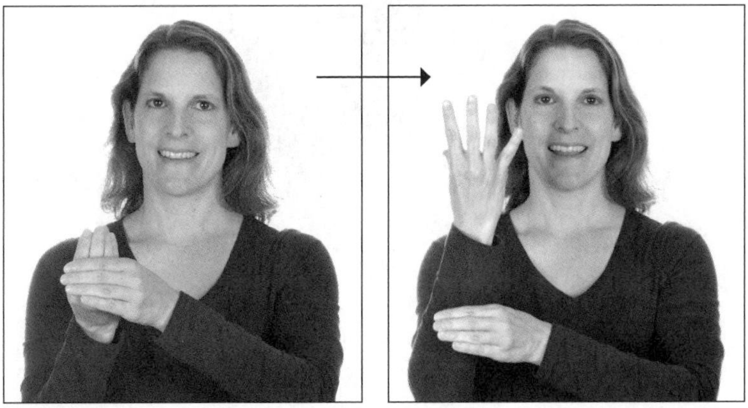

SPRING: Cup one hand and bring the other hand up through it, spreading the fingers as the hand "grows."

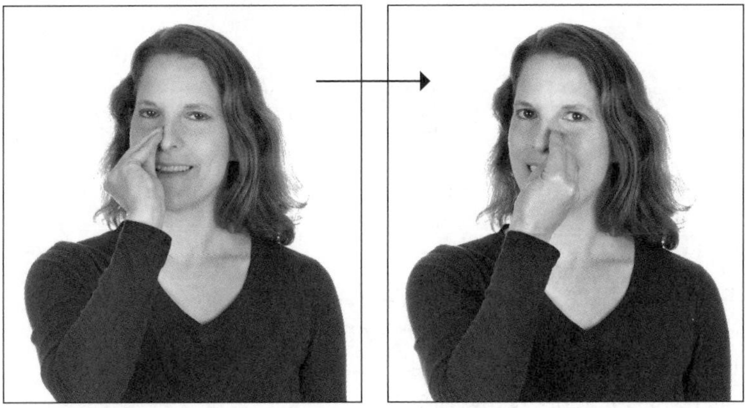

FLOWER: Bring gathered index fingers and thumb to one side of the nose and then the other, as if smelling a flower.

I-LOVE-YOU: Hold up thumb, index finger, and pinky.

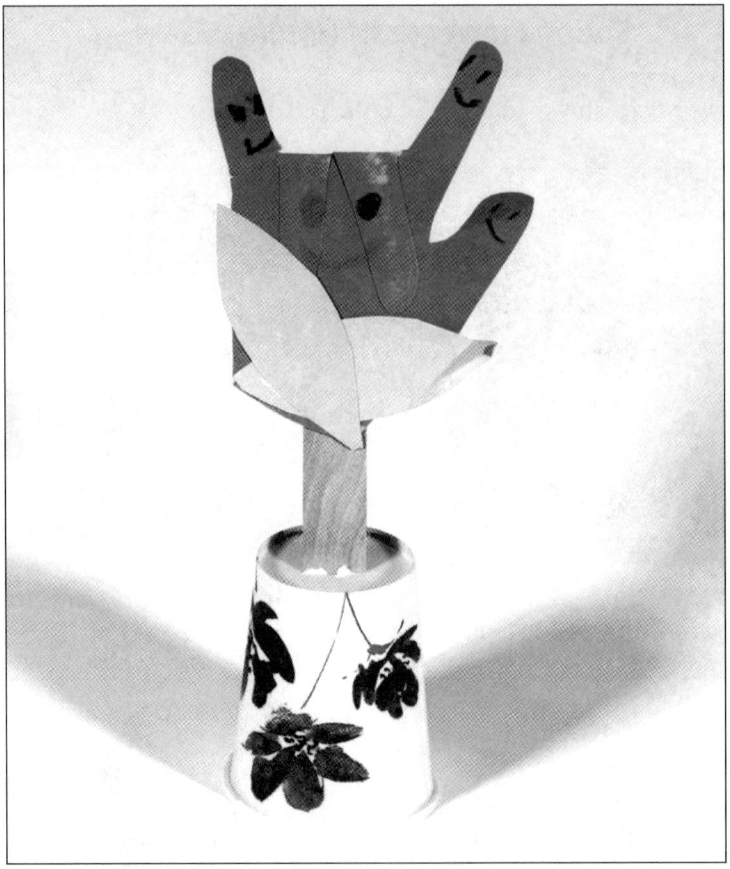

Directions:

1. Trace a hand on construction paper and cut it out.
2. Glue down the middle and ring fingers of the hand so that it forms the sign I-LOVE-YOU.
3. Decorate the hand as desired.
4. Tape one end of a craft stick or straw to the back of the I-LOVE-YOU hand.
5. Cut out leaves from green construction paper and tape them to the craft stick or straw.
6. Use a pencil to punch a hole in the bottom of a paper cup.
7. Place the straw in the hole and pull it down so that the I-LOVE-YOU flower is hidden.
8. Push the craft stick or straw up from the bottom to make your flower grow! When you are ready to display your craft, turn the cup over to form a flowerpot. Poke the craft stick or straw through the hole to display.

Why It Works

Even toddlers can complete this simple craft if you precut the pieces. Using safety scissors to cut out the pieces assists older children in developing fine motor skills. This is a great craft for sharing some of your signs with other family members!

A NOTE ABOUT THE SIGNS

The sign I-LOVE-YOU is also an informal way to say "Thanks so much!" or "You're terrific." The handshape for this sign can often be difficult for very young children, so don't be surprised if it takes them a little while to get it right!

READ AND SIGN TOGETHER!

For Babies and Toddlers

Baby Loves Spring! by Karen Katz. New York: Little Simon, 2012.
My Spring Robin by Anne Rockwell. New York: Macmillan, 1989.
Mouse's First Spring by Lauren Thompson. New York: Simon and Schuster, 2005.

For Preschoolers

Splish, Splash, Spring by Jan Carr. New York: Holiday House, 2001.
Signs of Spring by Justine Fontes. New York: Mondo, 2002.
Hurray for Spring by Patricia Hubbell. Minnetonka, MN: NorthWord, 2005.

Where Is Baby's Beach Ball? (ages birth to three years)

In this colorful board book by Karen Katz (New York: Little Simon, 2009), a baby searches under and around objects at the beach for her lost beach ball. Babies will love to lift the big, sturdy flaps and find the surprises underneath!

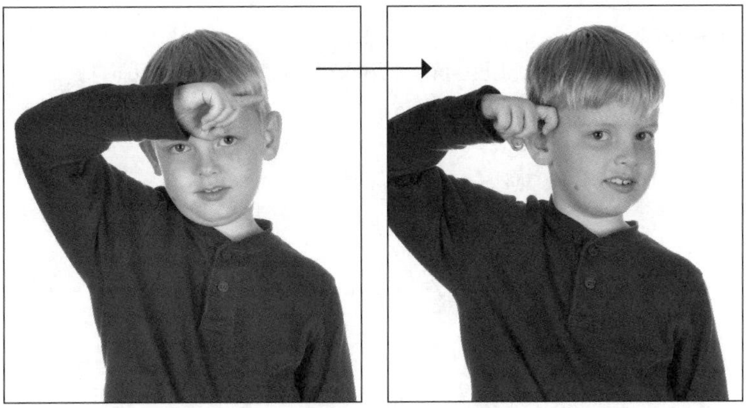

SUMMER: Draw your index finger sideways across your forehead, curling it as it moves, to represent wiping sweat away.

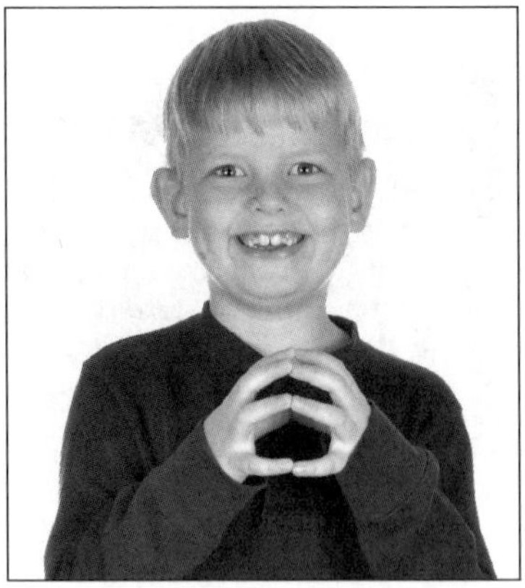

BALL: Hold two claw-handshapes together as if holding a ball.

WHERE: With your palm facing out and your eyebrows furrowed, move your index finger from side to side.

Why It Works

Sturdy cardboard books like this one are ideal for babies, and the lift-the-flap format engages children by adding an element of suspense. As you read the story, use signs to ask "Where is the ball?" on each page, and then invite your child to lift the flap. Extend the story by looking over the pictures afterward and asking your child to point out other objects.

READ AND SIGN TOGETHER!

For Babies and Toddlers

Welcome Summer by Jill Ackerman. New York: Scholastic, 2010.

Kipper's Sunny Day by Mick Inkpen. New York: Harcourt, 2001.

Mouse's First Summer by Lauren Thompson. New York: Simon and Schuster, 2004.

For Preschoolers

Sea, Sand, Me! by Patricia Hubbell. New York: HarperCollins, 2001.

Now It Is Summer by Eileen Spinelli. Grand Rapids, MI: Eerdmans Books for Young Readers, 2011.

Summer Days and Nights by Wong Herbert Yee. New York: Henry Holt, 2012.

chapter 8

Concepts

AS CHILDREN MOVE CLOSER TO THE SCHOOL YEARS and become developmentally ready to read, they need to be exposed to explicit pre-reading concepts, such as the letters of the alphabet. The foundation is laid implicitly throughout the preschool years, whenever you talk, sign, or sing in an engaging way about numbers, colors, opposites, and other concepts. In this chapter, we focus on three important early learning concept areas: the alphabet, numbers one through ten, and colors.

ABCs

The Manual Alphabet (ages one to six years)

Why It Works

You can begin exposing your child to the manual alphabet as early as you like—think of it as another tool for increasing your child's letter knowledge. As your child gets older, fingerspelling offers even more benefits. Jan C. Hafer and Robert M. Wilson (1986), authors of some of the earliest research on the benefits of signing with hearing children, found that use of the manual alphabet with hearing children increased their motivation to learn letters and words and helped them differentiate words with similar patterns. These benefits come about because fingerspelling allows children to "physically experience" each letter, creating a stronger sense of it in the brain. Dr. Marilyn Daniels (1996) points out that adults often write down information as a way to hold onto it and that young children can use fingerspelling for the same purpose long before they develop the fine motor skills for writing.

There are also more practical benefits to teaching your child the manual alphabet. When your beginning writer comes to you, wanting to know how to spell something while you are on the phone or having a conversation with a friend, all you have to do is fingerspell while your conversation continues uninterrupted.

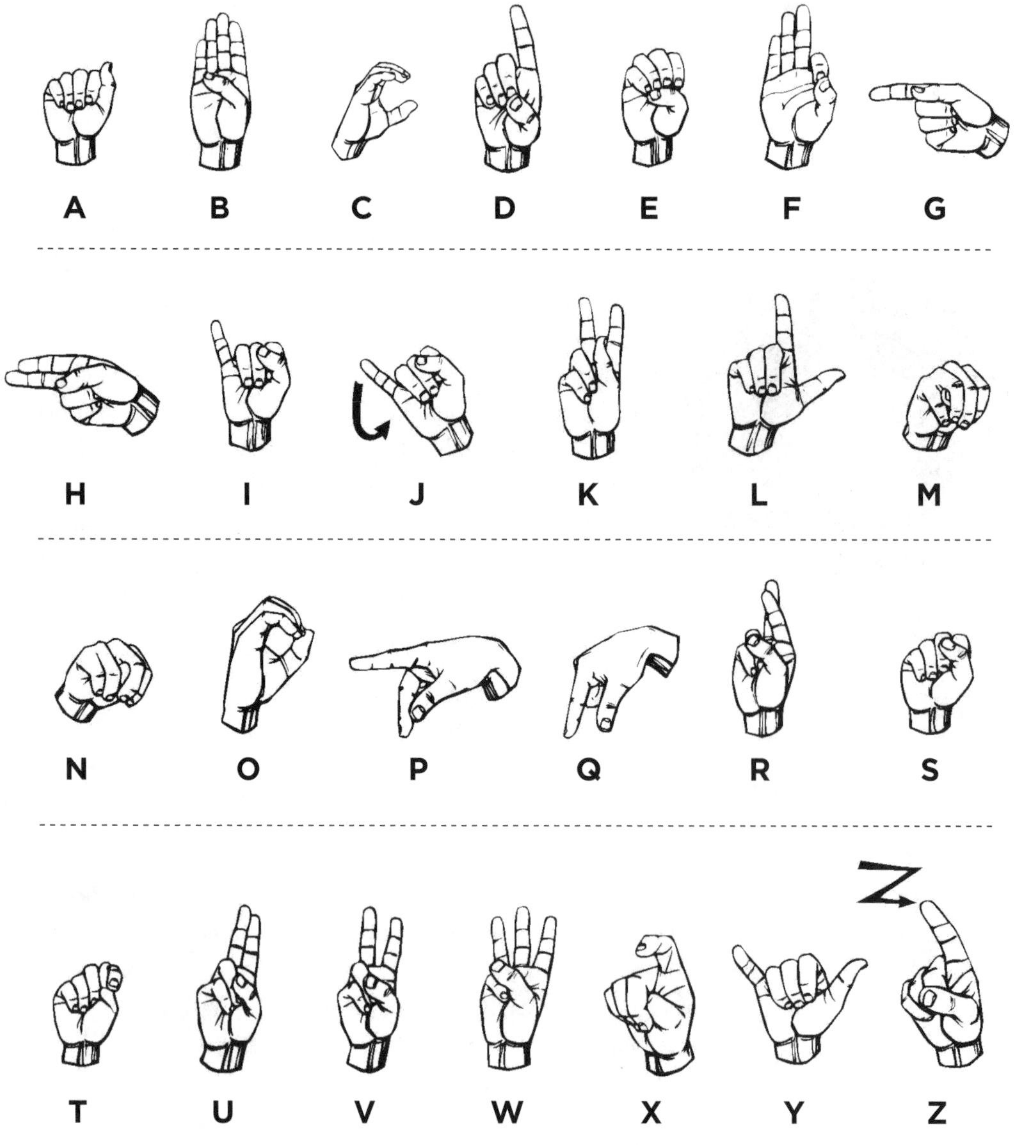

The Alphabet Game (ages three to six years)

This game can be played with two or more players. The first player signs a letter of the alphabet. The second must say a word that begins with that letter. Then the second player signs a letter and the first says a word, and so on.

Why It Works

This is a great waiting room or road trip game, as the only materials needed are your hands and brain! Though the game is simple, it fosters playful interaction with your child and reinforces the manual alphabet and letter sounds.

Letter of the Day (ages two to six years)

Emphasize alphabetic knowledge by choosing a letter of the day! If you have alphabet refrigerator magnets, dump them all into a bag and let your child choose one to be the special featured letter. Then sign that letter together and discuss the sound it makes. Celebrate the letter all day long with some of these activities:

- Draw the letter in the air with your finger.
- Make a list of words that begin with the letter.
- Cut the letter out of construction paper.
- Mold the letter with clay or beeswax.
- Spray shaving cream or whipped cream onto a plate and use your finger to write the letter in the cream.
- Use a stick to scratch the letter in the dirt.
- When you go out, look for words that begin with the letter on roadside signs.
- Explore the sounds that the letter makes. Whenever you hear or say a word that begins with the letter, sign it!
- Ask your local librarian to suggest alliterative picture books that feature the letter.

Why It Works

The more you engage your child and all her senses, the more she will learn! Toddlers and young children are very interested in social cues—they find things interesting because other people do. So if you show that the alphabet is important, then your child will think it is too. And all the while you will be supporting letter knowledge and phonemic awareness, both important predictors of reading success.

Name Plaques (ages three to six years)

Directions:

1. Photocopy the manual alphabet sheet from appendix C. If a letter appears more than once in your child's name, print enough sheets to give you the correct number of letters.
2. Cut out the letters and lay them out on the table.
3. Help your child find the letters of his name. Sign the letters and help him compare them to the shapes in the pictures until he finds the correct ones.
4. Glue the letters onto the construction paper or cardstock to make the name.
5. Decorate as desired with crayons, markers, and stickers.

Why It Works

Being able to read letters is just as important as knowing how to write them. Recognizing the sounds of letters is just as important as being able to produce the sounds. And recognizing the manual alphabet is just as important as knowing how to sign it. This activity gives your child practice in recognizing the shapes of the letters and distinguishing them from one another. If your child is overwhelmed by the pile of letters and doesn't know where to begin, pull out two letters and focus his attention on them. Sign the letter you are looking for and ask him to tell you whether the letters on the paper are the same or different. Repeat until you have found all the letters of his name. This kind of modeling helps your child learn how to break down complex tasks into manageable chunks. Letting him do as much of the work as he can, however, is an important part of the process, as it helps him develop critical thinking skills and confidence.

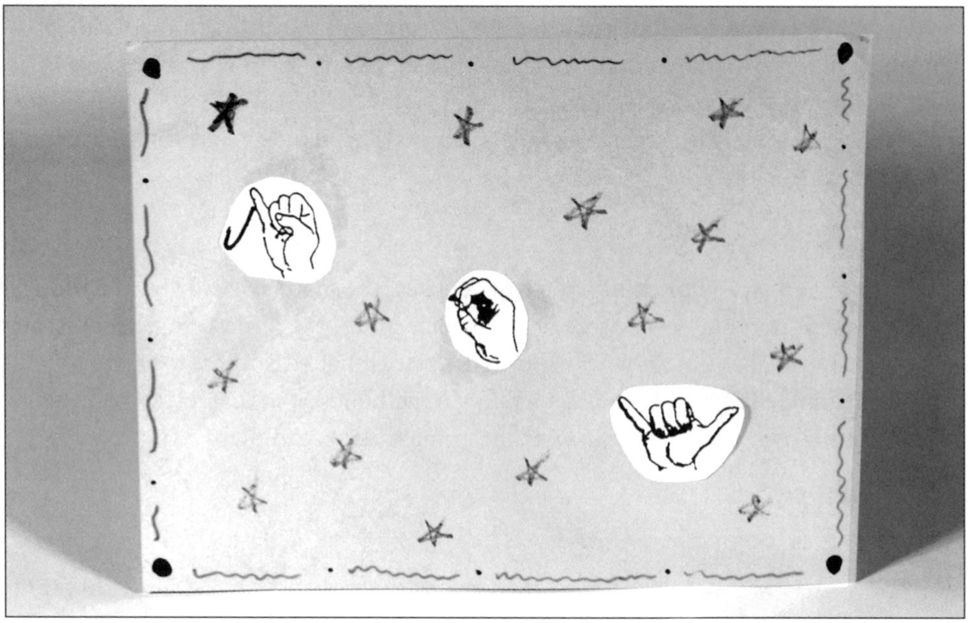

READ AND SIGN TOGETHER!

For Babies and Toddlers

Handsigns: A Sign Language Alphabet by Kathleen Fain. San Francisco: Chronicle, 1993.

ABC for You and Me by Meg Girnis. Morton Grove, IL: Albert Whitman, 2000.

Chicka Chicka Boom Boom by Bill Martin Jr. New York: Simon and Schuster, 1989.

For Preschoolers

The Turn-Around, Upside-Down Alphabet Book by Lisa Campbell Ernst. New York: Simon and Schuster, 2004.

The Handmade Alphabet by Laura Rankin. New York: Dial, 1991.

Albert's Alphabet by Leslie Tryon. New York: Aladdin, 1994.

Numbers

My Bouncing Buckaroo (ages birth to two years)

(traditional)

ONE I love you, TWO I love you,
THREE I LOVE you so.
FOUR I love you, FIVE I love you,
Rock you to and fro.
SIX I love you, SEVEN I love you,
EIGHT you LOVE me too!
NINE I love you, TEN I love you,
My bouncing buckaroo!

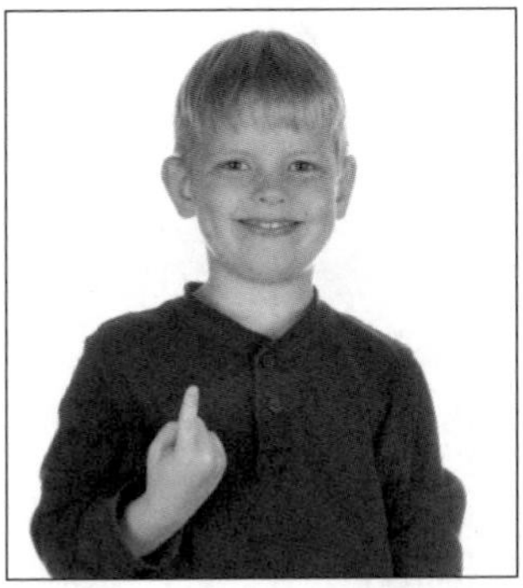

ONE: Hold up index finger with palm facing you.

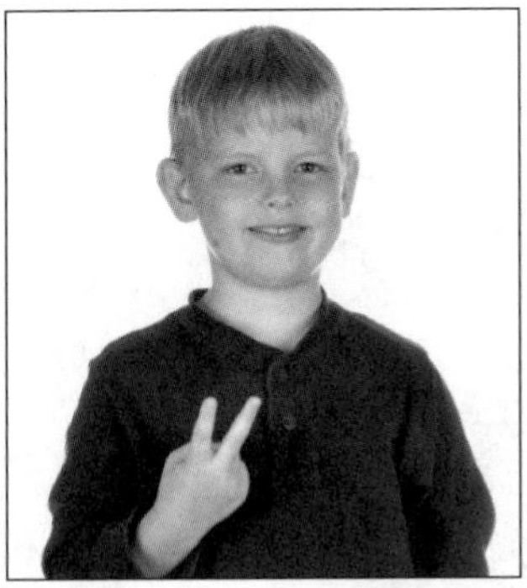

TWO: Hold up index and middle fingers with palm facing you.

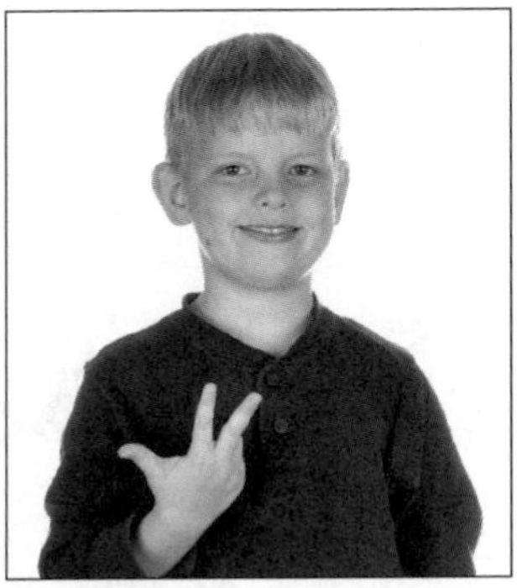

THREE: Hold up index and middle fingers and thumb with palm facing you.

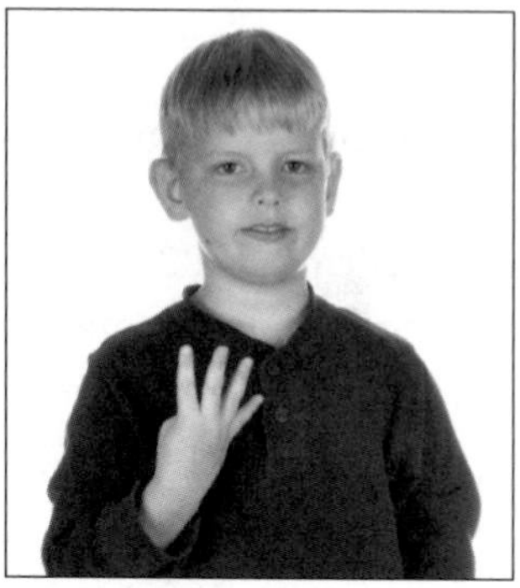

FOUR: Hold up all four fingers with palm facing you.

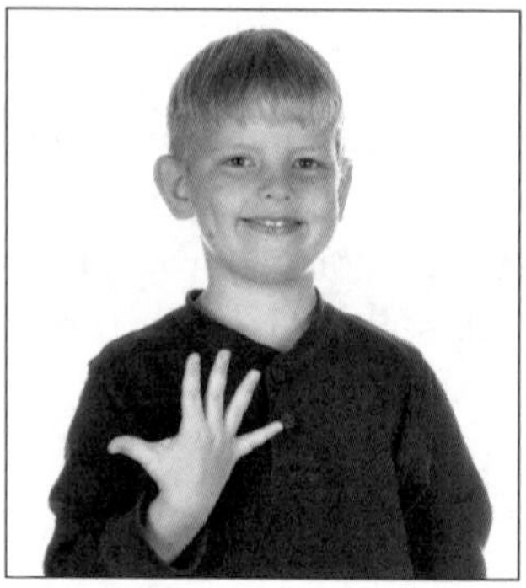

FIVE: Hold up all four fingers and thumb with palm facing you.

SIX: Hold up your hand with your palm facing away from you and touch your thumb to your pinky.

SEVEN: Hold up your hand with your palm facing away from you and touch your thumb to your ring finger.

EIGHT: Hold up your hand with your palm facing away from you and touch your thumb to your middle finger.

NINE: Hold up your hand with your palm facing away from you and touch your thumb to your index finger.

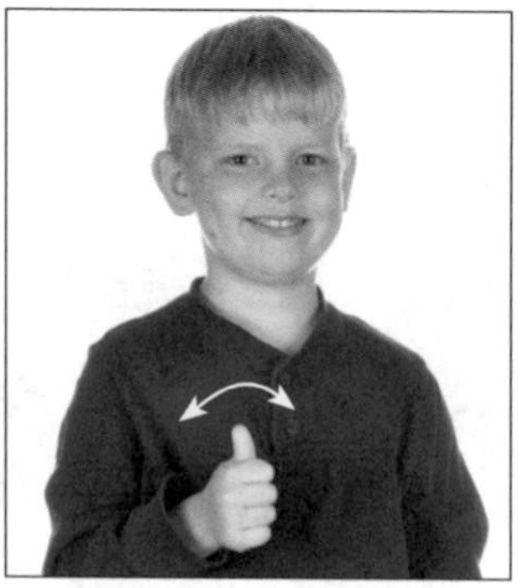

TEN: Hold up your thumb and twist your hand side to side.

LOVE: Cross fists over chest as if giving yourself a hug.

Why It Works

This traditional lap bounce has been engaging and calming babies for years. Little ones can't seem to resist the bouncy rhythms and the lovey-dovey message. (Plus, it's a great coincidence that when you sign LOVE with your baby on your lap, you're giving her a hug!) Slow down when you get to nine and ten to build up the suspense and increase your child's delight in the wild bounce at the end. In this rhyme, you are not only engaging your child or distracting a fussy baby—you are also introducing important number concepts and exposing her to the rhythms of spoken language.

Ten Friends: A Counting Rhyme (ages one to six years)

ONE is fun, But TWO is better.
THREE friends, FOUR friends play together.
FIVE friends are here now, and more!
Number SIX comes through the door.
Now SEVEN, EIGHT, NINE, and then
Another friend comes in—it's TEN!
TEN good friends to run and play
And count together every day!

Why It Works

Learning to count in American Sign Language is not to be confused with counting on your fingers! Remind your child that this is counting in another language, just as if you were learning the Spanish or French words for the numbers. In fact, learning number names in any language can be difficult for children, as the names for numbers are nothing but arbitrary words (or signs) that represent a concept and must be listed in a certain order. That is why counting games, which offer repetition of the numbers in order, are a staple of childhood in every language.

READ AND SIGN TOGETHER!

For Babies and Toddlers

Ten, Nine, Eight by Molly Bang. New York: Greenwillow, 1993.
My Very First Book of Numbers by Eric Carle. New York: Philomel, 1974.
Counting Kisses by Karen Katz. New York: Margaret K. McElderry, 2001.

For Preschoolers

Ten Apples Up on Top! by Theo LeSieg. New York: Random House, 1961.
The Handmade Counting Book by Laura Rankin. New York: Dial, 1998.
Mouse Count by Ellen Stoll Walsh. San Diego, CA: Harcourt Brace, 1991.

Colors

I Spy (ages three to six years)

Play a variation on the traditional game to reinforce color vocabulary. Select an object in your surroundings and then say to your child, "I spy something _____." Sign the color. Let your child guess what the object is, encouraging him to describe items carefully. Model this in your own guesses—for example, by saying, "Is it the yellow butterfly next to the water fountain?" Then let your child have a turn.

Why It Works

This is a great waiting room game or car game. Kids of various ages can play together; older kids will be more inclined to participate because of the challenge of the signed vocabulary, and the game is well within the abilities of younger kids. Letting everyone have a turn promotes self-confidence and expressive language.

RED: Rub index finger downward over bottom lip.

ORANGE: Hold an O-handshape in front of your mouth and then squeeze as if squeezing an orange.

YELLOW: Hold up pinky and thumb to make a Y-handshape and then shake it.

GREEN: Hold up index finger and thumb to make a G-handshape and then shake it.

BLUE: Hold all four fingers together and fold thumb over palm to make a B-handshape and then shake it.

PURPLE: Hold up index and middle fingers and then touch thumb between them. Turn this shape upside-down to make a P-handshape and then shake it.

PINK: Hold up index and middle fingers and then touch thumb between them. Turn this shape upside-down to make a P-handshape and then rub the middle finger downward over your bottom lip.

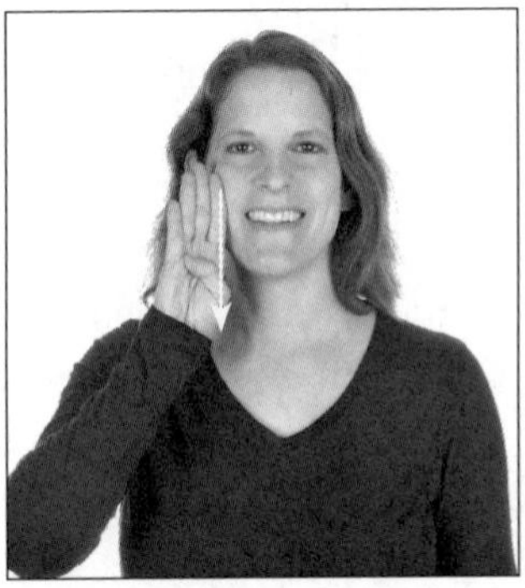

BROWN: Hold all four fingers together and fold thumb over palm to make a B-handshape. Move the B-handshape downward by your cheek.

GRAY: Hold your flat hands in front of you with the palms facing you. Move the hands alternately back and forth so that the fingers make contact.

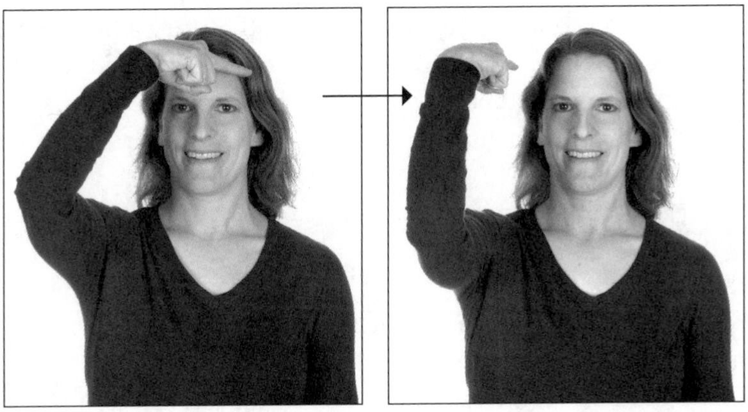

BLACK: Draw your index finger across your forehead.

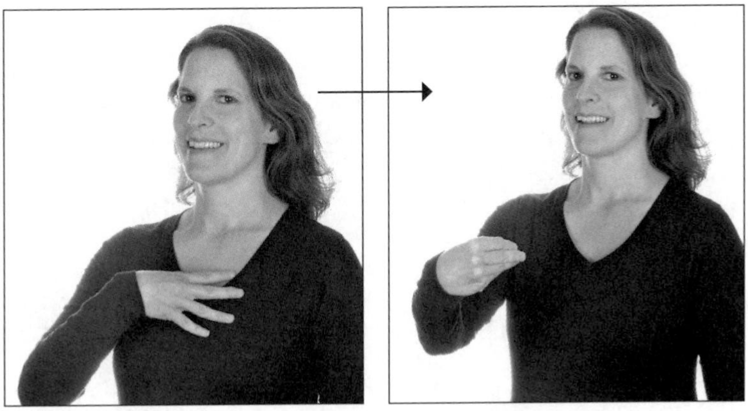

WHITE: Touch your fingers and thumb to your chest and then move your hand away from you, pulling your fingers together.

Dog's Colorful Day (ages one to six years)

In this book by Emma Dodd (New York: Puffin, 2000), Dog is white with a black spot on one ear, but when he goes exploring he gets all kinds of colorful spots on his coat! You can also share this story as a magnetboard story, either before, after, or instead of reading the actual book. Print out the pictures by artist Melanie Fitz from appendix C. Then cut out the dog and bathtub shapes and place adhesive magnets on the back. (Laminate or cover the pieces with contact paper first to make them more durable.) Make small circles of different colors and place magnets on the backs of those too. Then tell the story using these simple props and your refrigerator or file cabinet as a backdrop.

Why It Works

This is an excellent book to sign with, as it uses a repetitive structure and features one color concept per page. As you read the story, you can introduce or review color signs, ask your child to count the spots, and ask your child to predict what will happen next. All of these actions engage your child in the story and help her become aware of narrative structure in an organic way. Inviting your child to tell and retell the story through the magnetboard will develop her narrative skills. (And, let's be honest, keep her out of your hair while you're making dinner . . .)

READ AND SIGN TOGETHER!

For Babies and Toddlers

Baby's Colors by Karen Katz. New York: Little Simon, 2010.
I Love Colors by Margaret Miller. New York: Little Simon, 1999.
A Book of Colors by Kim Votry. Washington, DC: Gallaudet University Press, 2003.

For Preschoolers

Cat's Colors by Jane Cabrera. New York: Dial, 1997.
Pete the Cat: I Love My White Shoes by Eric Litwin. New York: Harper, 2008.
Mouse Paint by Ellen Stoll Walsh. San Diego, CA: Harcourt Brace, 1989.

appendix a

More Resources for Signing with Young Children

BOOKS AND ARTICLES

Ault, Kelly. *Let's Sign! Every Baby's Guide to Communicating with Grownups*. New York: Houghton Mifflin, 2005.

Bahan, Ben, and Joe Dannis. *Signs for Me: Basic Sign Vocabulary for Children, Parents, and Teachers*. San Diego, CA: DawnSignPress, 1990.

Beyer, Monica. *Baby Talk: A Guide to Using Basic Sign Language to Communicate with Your Baby*. New York: Penguin, 2006.

Beyer, Monica. *Teach Your Baby to Sign*. Beverly, MA: Fair Winds Press, 2007.

Bingham, Sara. *The Baby Signing Book*. Toronto, ON: Robert Rose, 2007.

Briant, Monta Z. *Baby Sign Language Basics*. Carlsbad, CA: Hay House, 2004.

Briant, Monta Z. *Sign, Sing, and Play! Fun Signing Activities for You and Your Baby*. Carlsbad, CA: Hay House, 2006.

Briant, Monta Z. and Susan Z. *Songs for Little Hands Activity Guide and CD*. Carlsbad, CA: Hay House, 2008.

Chafin, Suzie. *Baby Sign Language*. Guilford, CT: Morris Book Publishing, 2010.

Daniels, Marilyn. *Dancing with Words: Signing for Hearing Children's Literacy*. Westport, CT: Bergin and Garvey, 2001.

Dennis, Kirsten, and Tressa Azpiri. *Sign to Learn: American Sign Language in the Early Childhood Classroom*. St. Paul, MN: Redleaf Press, 2005.

Fixell, Andrea, and Ted Stafford. *Baby Signing: How to Talk with Your Baby in American Sign Language*. New York: Penguin, 2006.

Garcia, Joseph. *Sign with Your Baby: How to Communicate with Infants before They Can Speak*. Mukilteo, WA: Northlight Communications, 1999.

Kubler, Annie. *My First Signs*. Auburn, ME: Child's Play, 2005.

Kubler, Annie. *Sign and Singalong: Baa, Baa Black Sheep*. Auburn, ME: Child's Play, 2004.

Kubler, Annie. *Sign and Singalong: Itsy Bitsy Spider*. Auburn, ME: Child's Play, 2004.

Kubler, Annie. *Sign and Singalong: Teddy Bear, Teddy Bear*. Auburn, ME: Child's Play, 2004.

Kubler, Annie. *Sign and Singalong: Twinkle, Twinkle, Little Star*. Auburn, ME: Child's Play, 2004.

Malloy, Tiara V. "Sign Language Use for Deaf, Hard of Hearing, and Hearing Babies: The Evidence Supports It." American Society for Deaf Children, July 2003. http://ccc-manitoba.wikispaces.com/file/view/Sign+Language+Use-Evidence.pdf.

Miller, Anne Meeker. *Mealtime and Bedtime Sing and Sign*. Philadelphia, PA: Da Capo Press, 2008.

Miller, Anne Meeker. *Toddler Sing and Sign*. New York: Marlowe and Company, 2007.

Millman, Isaac. *Moses Goes to a Concert*. New York: Farrar, Straus and Giroux, 1998.

Millman, Isaac. *Moses Goes to a Play*. New York: Farrar, Straus and Giroux, 2004.

Millman, Isaac. *Moses Goes to School*. New York: Farrar, Straus and Giroux, 2000.

Millman, Isaac. *Moses Goes to the Circus*. New York: Farrar, Straus and Giroux, 2003.

Murray, Carol Garboden. *Simple Signing with Young Children: A Guide for Infant, Toddler, and Preschool Teachers*. Beltsville, MD: Gryphon House, 2007.

Taylor-DiLeva, Kim. *Once upon a Sign: Using American Sign Language to Engage, Entertain, and Teach All Children*. Santa Barbara, CA: Libraries Unlimited, 2011.

Thompson, Stacy A. *Teach Your Tot to Sign: The Parents' Guide to American Sign Language*. Washington, DC: Gallaudet University Press, 2005.

Votry, Kim. *Baby's First Signs*. Washington, DC: Gallaudet University Press, 2001.

Votry, Kim. *A Book of Colors*. Washington, DC: Gallaudet University Press, 2003.

Votry, Kim. *More Baby's First Signs*. Washington, DC: Gallaudet University Press, 2003.

Votry, Kim. *Out for a Walk*. Washington, DC: Gallaudet University Press, 2003.

Warner, Penny. *Baby's Favorite Rhymes to Sign*. New York: Three Rivers Press, 2010.

Wheeler, Cindy. *More Simple Signs*. New York: Viking, 1998.

Wheeler, Cindy. *Simple Signs*. New York: Viking, 1995.

WEBSITES WITH VIDEO SIGN DICTIONARIES

ASL Pro: www.aslpro.com

Signing Savvy: www.signingsavvy.com

Signing with Your Baby: www.signingbaby.com

DVDS

Sign Language Storytelling Series. Many favorite picture book titles available. New York: Scholastic, 2010 and on.

Signing Time! series. Many theme-based volumes available. Salt Lake City, UT: Signing Time Productions, 2002 to present.

Teaching Signs for Baby Minds Series. Vol. 1, *Everyday Signs*. Vol. 2, *Concepts and Combinations*. Vol. 3, *Dictionary and Alphabet*. Coos Bay, OR: Bright Minds, 2007.

appendix b

More Resources for Early Literacy and Child Development

Acredolo, Linda P., and Susan Goodwyn. *Baby Minds: Brain-Building Games Your Baby Will Love*. New York: Bantam Books, 2000.

Bailey, Becky A. *I Love You Rituals*. New York: HarperCollins, 2000.

Benjamin, Floella. *Skip across the Ocean: Nursery Rhymes from around the World*. New York: Orchard Books, 1995.

Blakemore, Caroline, and Barbara Weston Ramirez. *Baby Read-Aloud Basics*. New York: AMACOM, 2006.

Blythe, Sally Goddard. *The Well-Balanced Child: Movement and Early Learning*. Gloucestershire, UK: Hawthorn Press, 2006.

Gerber, Magda. *Dear Parent: Caring for Infants with Respect*. Los Angeles, CA: Resources for Infant Educarers, 2002.

Isbell, Christy. *Everyday Play: Fun Games to Develop the Fine Motor Skills Your Child Needs for School*. Silver Spring, MD: Gryphon House, 2010.

Mayes, Linda C., and Donald J. Cohen. *The Yale Child Study Center Guide to Understanding Your Child: Healthy Development from Birth to Adolescence*. Boston: Little, Brown, 2002.

Medina, John. *Brain Rules for Baby: How to Raise a Smart and Happy Child from Zero to Five*. Seattle, WA: Pear Press, 2010.

Opie, Iona, ed. *My Very First Mother Goose.* Cambridge, MA: Candlewick, 1996.

Parlakian, Rebecca. *Before the ABCs: Promoting School Readiness in Infants and Toddlers.* Washington, DC: Zero to Three, 2003.

Pica, Rae. *Jump into Literacy: Active Learning for Preschool Children.* Beltsville, MD: Gryphon House, 2007.

Ramey, Craig T., and Sharon L. Ramey. *Right from Birth: Building Your Child's Foundation for Life.* New York: Goddard Press, 1999.

Rawson, Martyn, and Michael Rose. *Ready to Learn: From Birth to School Readiness.* Gloucestershire, UK: Hawthorn Press, 2006.

Sasse, Margaret. *Active Baby, Healthy Brain.* New York: The Experiment, 2009.

Schiller, Pam. *The Complete Resource Book for Infants.* Beltsville, MD: Gryphon House, 2005.

Schiller, Pam. *Creating Readers.* Beltsville, MD: Gryphon House, 2001.

Shickedanz, Judith. *Much More Than the ABCs: The Early Stages of Reading and Writing.* Washington, DC: NAEYC, 1999.

Shonkoff, Jack P., and Deborah A. Phillips, eds. *From Neurons to Neighborhoods: The Science of Early Childhood Development.* Washington, DC: National Academy Press, 2000.

Stewart, David A., and Bryan R. Clarke. *Literacy and Your Deaf Child: What Every Parent Should Know.* Washington, DC: Gallaudet, 2003.

Weitzman, Elaine, and Janice Greenberg. *Learning Language and Loving It.* Toronto, ON: Hanen Centre, 2002.

appendix c

Craft Templates

Photocopy these patterns at 125 percent to fit on 8 ½ x 11 paper.

X

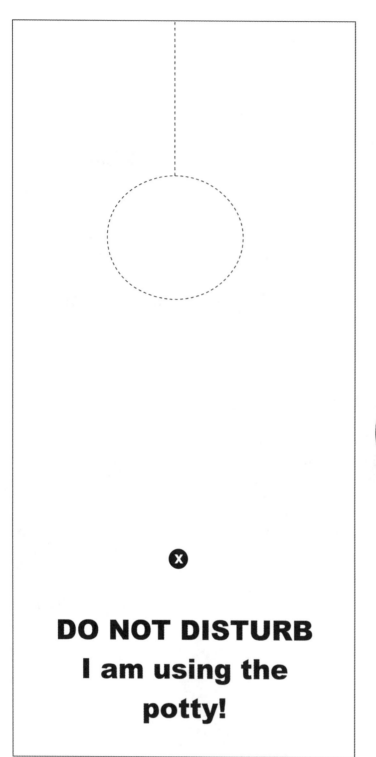

DO NOT DISTURB
I am using the potty!

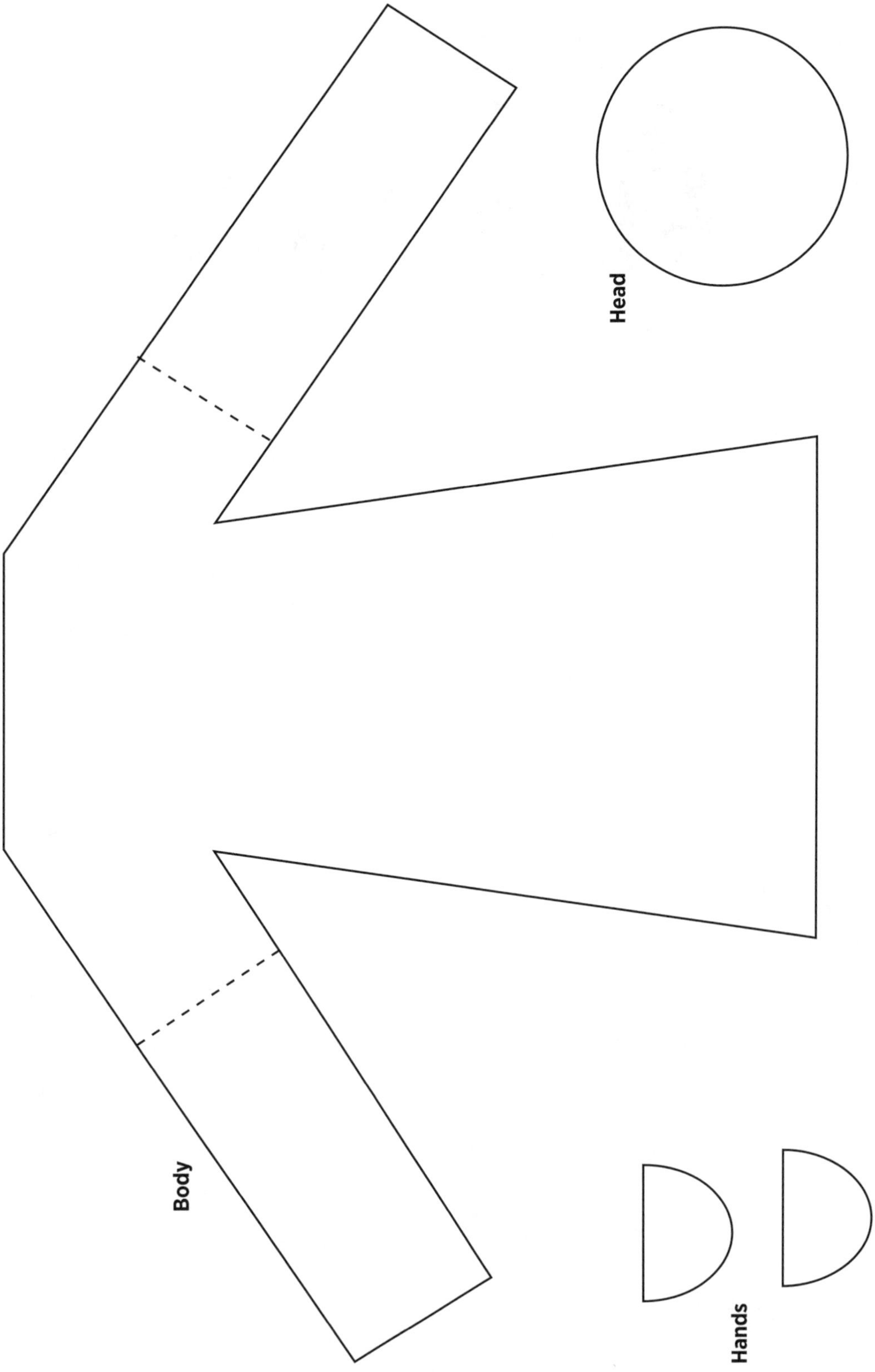
Head
Body
Hands

Today

I

will go to...

the library.

school.

the dentist.

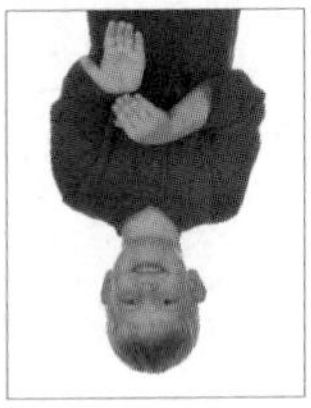

the doctor.

the post office.

a restaurant.

the playground.

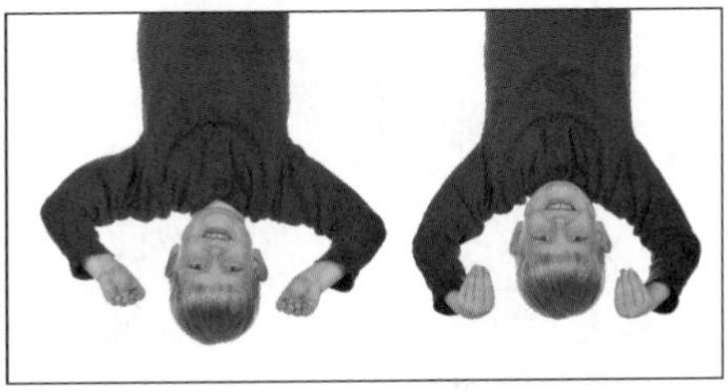

the store.

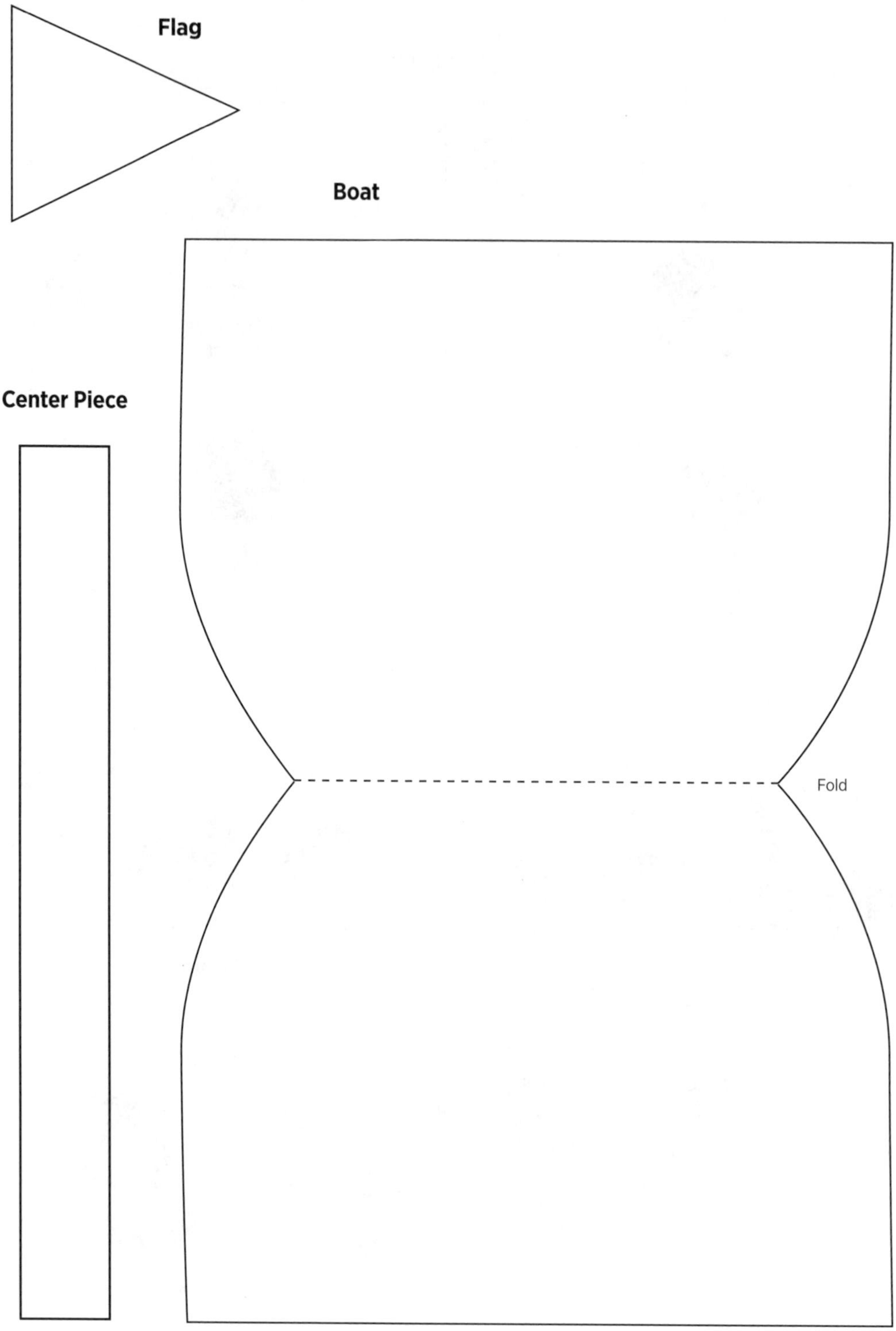
Flag
Boat
Center Piece
Fold

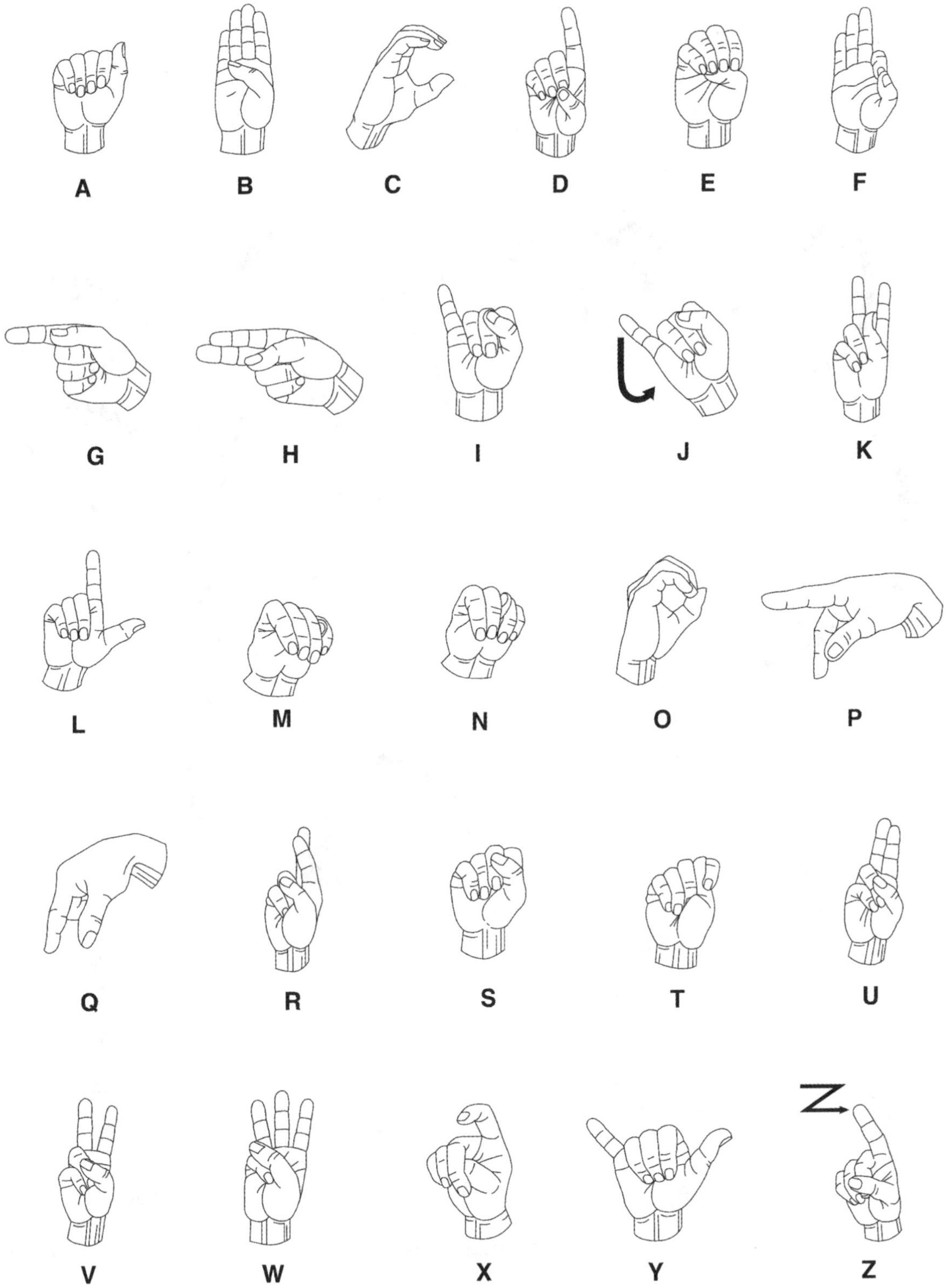

Manual Alphabet Sheet *(from page 110)*

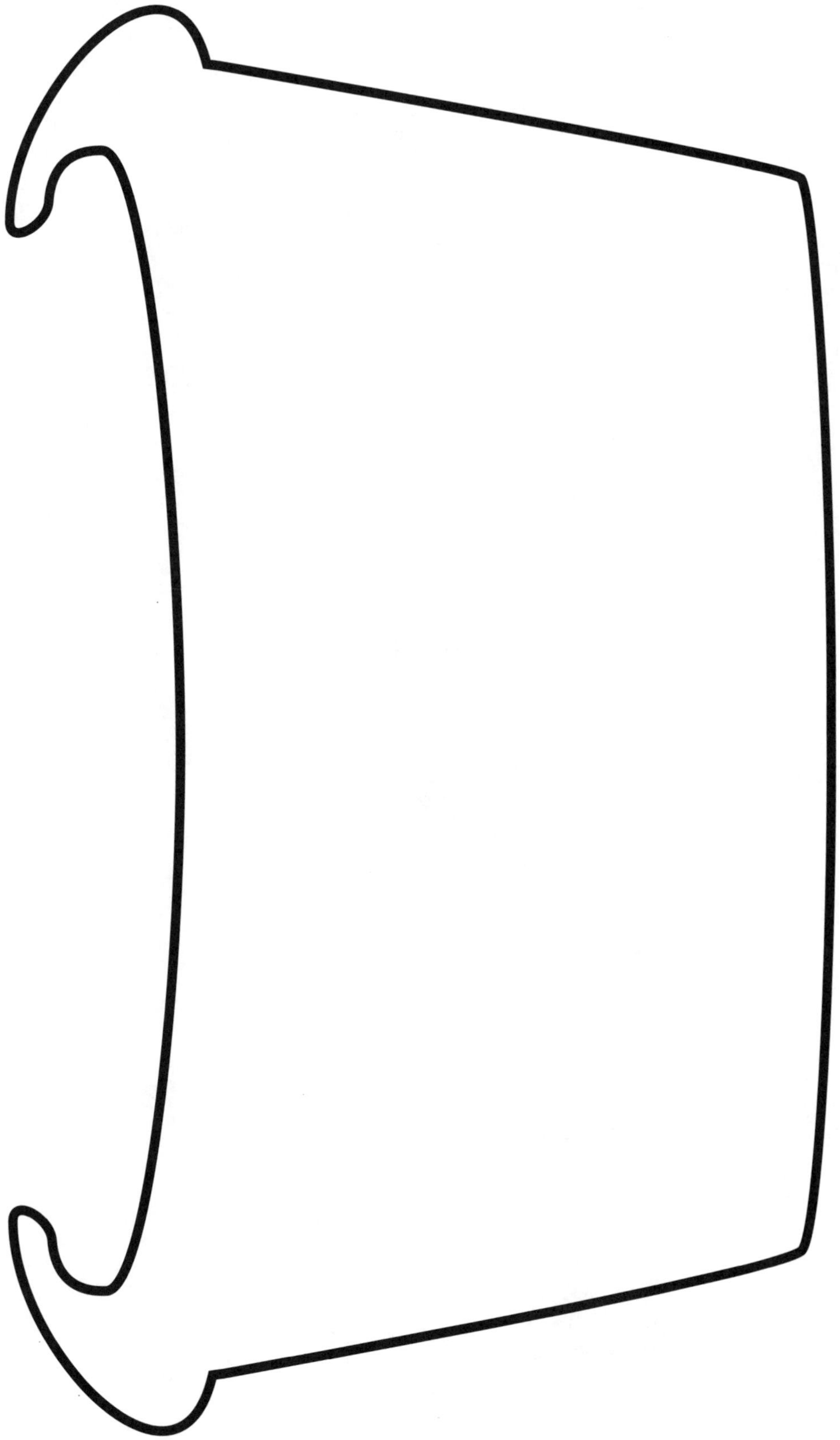

works cited

Bingham, Sara. 2007. *The Baby Signing Book*. Toronto, ON: Robert Rose.

Blakemore, Caroline J., and Barbara Weston Ramirez. 2006. *Baby Read-Aloud Basics*. New York: AMACOM.

Brady, Diane. 2000. "Look Who's Talking—with Their Hands." www.businessweek.com/2000/00_33/b3694165.htm?scriptFramed.

Briant, Monta Z. 2004. *Baby Sign Language Basics*. Carlsbad, CA: Hay House, 2004.

California School for the Deaf. 2005. *Early Childhood Education ASL Framework*. Fremont, CA: California School for the Deaf.

Daniels, Marilyn. 1996. "Seeing Language: The Effect Over Time of Sign Language on Vocabulary Development in Early Childhood Education." *Child Study Journal* 26 (March): 193.

Daniels, Marilyn. 2001. *Dancing with Words: Signing for Hearing Children's Literacy*. Westport, CT: Bergin and Garvey.

Daniels, Marilyn. 2003. "Using a Signed Language as a Second Language for Kindergarten Students." *Child Study Journal* 33 (January): 53.

Frazier-Maiwald, Virginia, and Lenore M. Williams. 1999. *Keys to Raising a Deaf Child*. Hauppage, NY: Barron's.

French, Martha M. 1999. *Starting with Assessment: A Developmental Approach to Deaf Children's Literacy*. Washington, DC: Gallaudet University.

Garcia, Joseph. 1999. *Sign with Your Baby: How to Communicate with Infants before They Can Speak*. Mukilteo, WA: Northlight Communications.

Ghoting, Saroj Nadkarni, and Pamela Martin-Diaz. 2005. *Early Literacy Storytimes @ your library*. Chicago, IL: American Library Association.

Hafer, Jan C., and Robert M. Wilson. 1986. *Signing for Reading Success*. Washington, DC: Kendall Green.

Isbell, Christy. 2010. *Everyday Play: Fun Games to Develop the Fine Motor Skills Your Child Needs for School*. Silver Spring, MD: Gryphon House.

Johnson, Susan R. 2007. "You and Your Child's Health: Teaching Our Children to Write, Read, and Spell." www.youandyourchildshealth.org.

Mayes, Linda C., and Donald J. Cohen. 2002. *The Yale Child Study Center Guide to Understanding Your Child: Healthy Development from Birth to Adolescence*. Boston: Little, Brown.

Miller, Anne Meeker. 2007. *Toddler Sing and Sign*. New York: Marlowe.

Ontario Ministry of Children and Youth Services. 2010. Services for Children Who Are Deaf or Hard of Hearing: Developmental Milestones in American Sign Language (ASL). www.children.gov.on.ca/htdocs/English/topics/earlychildhood/hearing/brochure_services.aspx.

Sasse, Margaret. 2009. *Active Baby, Healthy Brain*. New York: The Experiment.

Shelov, Steven, and Tanya Remer Altmann, eds. 2009. *Caring for Your Baby and Young Child: Birth to Age 5*. 5th ed. American Academy of Pediatrics. New York: Bantam.

Shonkoff, Jack P., and Deborah A. Phillips, eds. 2000. *From Neurons to Neighborhoods: The Science of Early Childhood Development*. Washington, DC: National Academy Press.

Weitzman, Elaine, and Janice Greenberg. 2002. *Learning Language and Loving It*. Toronto, ON: Hanen Centre.

Zero to Three. 2003. "Early Literacy." www.zerotothree.org/child-development/early-language-literacy/earlyliteracy2pagehandout.pdf.

index of activities by age

Because every child develops at his or her own pace, the recommended ages are simply a guideline. You are the best judge of what will engage your child.

INFANTS (AGES BIRTH TO TWELVE MONTHS)

YOUNGER TODDLERS (AGES ONE TO TWO YEARS)

(continued on page 136)

YOUNGER TODDLERS (AGES ONE TO TWO YEARS, CONTINUED)

OLDER TODDLERS (AGES TWO TO THREE YEARS)

PRESCHOOLERS (AGES THREE TO SIX YEARS)

signs index

general index